P9-CQF-631

Dear Sarah,

Today is your birthday. It was almost three decades ago this morning that an Arkansas doctor drove in during an ice storm to deliver you. I heard you cry, and then he handed you to me and said, "Allow me to introduce you to your daughter." I made a vow then and there that I would never abandon you.

In truth, there are days when I think of the very real possibility of an early departure, and I am saddened by the thought of being separated from you. But I want you to know this: wherever I go, in this life or beyond its finite boundaries, my love for you will always be. Because since your birth, I have discovered that love is forever. Everything else will come to an end, even the universe, I am told, but not love, because love is who God is, and God is eternal.

—*adapted from the book*

Waiting for Bluebonnets

Letters to My Daughter

About God's Love

BOB LIVELY

DIMENSIONS
FOR LIVING
NASHVILLE

WAITING FOR BLUEBONNETS
LETTERS TO MY DAUGHTER ABOUT GOD'S LOVE

Copyright © 2004 by Robert D. Lively.

All rights reserved.
No part of this work may be reproduced or transmitted in any form or by any means, electronic or mechanical, including photocopying and recording, or by any information storage or retrieval system, except as may be expressly permitted by the 1976 Copyright Act or in writing from the publisher. Requests for permission should be addressed in writing to Dimensions for Living, 201 Eighth Avenue South, Nashville, TN 37203; or to permissions@abingdonpress.com.

This book is printed on acid-free paper.

Library of Congress Cataloging-in-Publication Data

Lively, Robert Donald.
  Waiting for bluebonnets : letters to my daughter about God's love / Bob Lively.
    p. cm.
  ISBN 0-687-34650-9 (pbk. : alk. paper)
  1. Meditations. I. Title.
  BV4832.3.L58 2004
  242'.4—dc22

                                                    2004016326

All scripture quotations unless noted otherwise are from the New Revised Standard Version of the Bible, copyright © 1989, by the Division of Christian Education of the National Council of the Churches of Christ in the United States of America. Used by permission. All rights reserved.

Scripture quotations noted RSV are from the Revised Standard Version of the Bible, copyright 1946, 1952, 1971 by the Division of Christian Education of the National Council of the Churches of Christ in the United States of America. Used by permission. All rights reserved.

04 05 06 07 08 09 10 11 12 13—10 9 8 7 6 5 4 3 2 1

MANUFACTURED IN THE UNITED STATES OF AMERICA

Contents

Introduction

TWO WEEKS AND ONE DAY AFTER THE TERRORIST ATTACKS ON THE World Trade Center and the Pentagon, I walked into the emergency room of North Austin Medical Center. An hour later, I was admitted to the hospital with a diagnosis of severe congestive heart failure. I'd seldom been ill. I'd always been a runner, hiker, basketball player, and long-distance walker, but on September 26, my life changed.

The cardiologist informed me that the disease was potentially deadly. In fact, he said, I was so sick that I might not have more than a short time to live. I will never forget the frown that covered his face like a pall when he said, "This thing could get very bad, very bad, indeed."

I lay alone in my hospital bed for five days waiting for "this thing" to get bad or for some sense of healing. I decided to allow myself to "feel" my feelings, as I was taught to say during my two years of clinical residency as a pastoral counselor. I carefully examined every feeling that slipped into my fuzzy awareness. I was not afraid, but I discovered that I was very sad because I realized that I would miss those I love.

Sarah Alice is the only child of two parents who are both professionals. In the close to thirty years I have been privileged to be her imperfect father, she has been a constant light in my life. On the morning of her graduation *magna cum laude* from St. Edward's University, my biweekly column in the *Austin American-Statesman* was an open letter to her. In that letter, I praised her accomplishments and thanked her for teaching me how to be a father. I knew in that hospital room that Sarah and I had a good bit of work still to do—not the least of which was for me to officiate at her wedding and sometime later to dote on her children and, once they were old enough, to teach them how to fish. There were also stories to tell her and her offspring, songs to sing, memories to make, and more love to share than my disease-induced fatigue would permit me to hope for in the hospital.

I don't remember much about those five days in the hospital, but I do recall the Saturday afternoon Sarah and I spent alone. As I stared at the dull ceiling, I longed to share with her what a light her beautiful spirit had always been. Even when she disagreed with me or my point of view, I celebrated the light that burns in her vibrant, adventurous spirit. Her tears, though, communicated the mystery connecting our two souls, and the depth of that mystery transcended mere words. Wisdom won, and I said nothing.

Two weeks later, I sat beneath a tree in shade provided by a generous October. In that hospitable place, as I waited for a friend, I prayed for the sense of purpose I had prior to the advent of this disease. Because I could think of nothing better to do after my brief prayer, I pulled out a notepad and jotted down a poem of sorts. When I finished, I recalled these words from the Christian mystic Meister Eckehart: "God is closer to me than I am to myself."

I've long found Eckehart's idea intriguing, and yet, until I became so ill, I hadn't really known what it meant to be close to myself, much less to the Divine. Today, though, I have a strong, experiential sense of both realities, and, even more, I now know that it is God who fills the gaps in my awareness and who mysteriously holds my fractured being together.

I decided that afternoon that I would tell my daughter of my nearly inexpressible love for her in a collection of letters. Because I was convinced that Meister Eckehart was right in his assessment of the proximity of God to us mere mortals, I would tell her about my more than fifty years of interacting with the Spirit in the humble cause of telling her what I'd learned about the power of love to heal us. To write to her of the truth of the palpable Mystery most of us call God, I felt that I should use a first-person perspective and the forms that are most often found in Scripture—poetry and stories. I was sufficiently encouraged by the letters and comments I received about the open letter I wrote to her to believe that this collection of letters might resonate with a sense of universality.

These letters, then, are for Sarah, but they also form a mosaic of God's kingdom for every reader who shares them with her. Some are poignant, some are meant to be funny, and some are simply memories that illustrate a facet of God's amazing and relentless determination to liberate us from a never-satisfying bondage to ourselves.

The response to that column was overwhelming. Readers throughout Central Texas wrote and called to say that what I had written about my relationship with my daughter had given them great comfort. A few went as far as to say that they were inspired by the column not to give up on the challenge of being a loving parent.

When I wrote the first letter in this collection, I was not at all certain that I would live long enough to produce more than a dozen or so. But by the power of grace and because of efficacious medical care, I have lived for six months—that span separating autumn from the first bloom of the bluebonnets in my beloved Texas Hill Country. At this milestone, I smile so vigorously sometimes that my face literally aches, for as I lay on my back in that austere hospital room, I asked God to permit me to see the bluebonnets one last time. These beautiful first flowers appeared on the foggy March morning I finished the last letter. In celebration of their azure magnificence, I composed one final one before hearing my soul whisper a benediction over this effort.

With every letter I composed, I realized increasingly that this work and this life have very little to do with me. The great mystery of human existence is that our lives are never really about us, but are given to us with the divine intention that we make of them reflections of our Source, who is inexplicably also our Destiny.

By God's grace, I have completed what I began beneath that tree in October. This work is personal, but in truth, it is not really about me. Although the memories are mine and the letters reflect my perceptions of glory, this collection is an imprecise picture of the kingdom Jesus proclaimed. The God about whom I write is the Person and the Power of my subjective experience. Subjectivity is the only way any of us can ever engage and really know the Mystery Holiness insists on remaining.

I am grateful to have lived long enough to produce this collection. My health has improved dramatically—even beyond the expectations of the physicians. I rejoice in this news because I have only very recently learned to get out of my way and, even more important, to get out of God's way. The fruit of this lesson has proved so personally rewarding that I am eager—but no longer in a hurry—to see what heaven has in mind for me next.

This collection is not about me, but is what every good piece of spiritual writing should be about—the healing properties of love.

March 2002

The Kindness of October

Dear Sarah,

As I lingered in a spot of shade created by a kind October, I celebrated with tears dropping as if by measure into a silence discovered only beyond the culture's stock expressions of joy.

I inhaled life and then prayed to a Mystery that as a child I was taught to view as triune, as though constructs might explain what we are never to know. As autumn gave rest to grass baked by the Texas summer and destined soon to become a leafy carpet where snow and ice would seldom visit, I was reminded of death. Even so, I happened upon a bud of hope rooted deep inside my loamy soul, and I found it in that plowed and broken acre separating the sum of my regrets from an ancient covenant sealed in blood.

The sweet fragrance of renewal summoned me beyond the disease that had invaded my being, and it generously welcomed me home like the prodigal that I am. From dappled shade I heard whispered the only word that ever matters, and, strangely, it came to me as a question: "Heaven?"

"Not just yet," I replied audaciously, as though I owned a vote in the issue. "You see, I have this thing to write for my daughter," I explained, as if an explanation might sway the decision. And, much like grace, my answer appeared to suffice, at least for this day.

Before I closed my prayer with a little "amen," I dared to ask again that I might see the bluebonnets bloom in the Hill Country at least one last time.

—Dad

On Top of a Mountain

Dear Sarah,

I LEARNED, EVEN BEFORE I COULD READ, OF A MAN NAMED Abraham who was called upon by God to take his child, a little boy like I was when I first heard this story, to the top of a high mountain. The only mountain I'd been on when I first heard this ancient tale was Pikes Peak. I'd ridden to its cold, bare summit in a train of passenger cars pulled by a steam locomotive while my father held me in his arms.

Once on top, I am told that I reported that I felt funny, and I suspect it was because I'd never before experienced 14,000 feet above sea level. Soon after whispering this primitively expressed symptom, I fainted in my father's arms. He carried me inside a warm building called the Summit House and poured warm cocoa down me until I regained consciousness, strength, and, most of all, the confidence to make the trip down.

On the slow, smoky descent, I pondered fainting. I didn't know we human beings could do such a thing as faint. But I was only four at the time, and I figured that there was much to learn about this life, and fainting would be but one of many lessons.

Months later in a Presbyterian kindergarten, I was told of a God who commanded a man, a father like my own dad, to slay his little boy. Even though I'd just turned five, I decided that I would not believe in a God who would require a father to sacrifice his son. I much preferred a God who was more like my dad. I didn't know much, but I recognized that I needed a God who would hold me and whisper reassurances as he poured warm cocoa into me when I was weak, scared, and confused.

Years later I would learn that the one Jesus called Father—or "Daddy," which is closer to the actual translation of *Abba*—loved me more than even my father loved me. I would not understand the story of Abraham and his little boy until I, too, was a father—*your* father, Sarah. And the point it makes is this: the One who loves us and reassures us was perfectly willing to do exactly what he commanded Abraham to do, although he was not about to permit Abraham to follow through with it. Centuries later Jesus' Father did follow through, and his beloved Son, the incarnation of perfect love, was nailed to a Roman cross.

As much as I love you, Sarah, I know that I will never understand that kind of love. The power of it has baffled me for a lifetime—and comforted me every time I was weak, scared, and confused.

—Dad

Surrender

Dear Sarah,

FEWER THAN TWENTY MILES FROM UNCLE WILL'S FARM, A COLD spring bubbled out of the ironstone in the shade provided by a stand of loblolly pines. Next to this pristine pool someone had erected what appeared to be a homemade sign that bore this reverent and likely apocryphal little reminder: "Davy Crockett and his Tennesseans drank from these very waters on their trek to the Alamo."

Utter the word *Alamo* in the hearing of anyone born in Texas, and something deep, even mysterious, happens inside that person. The word *holy*, which means "set apart from the mundane," comes closest to describing the depth of the respect that every reference to the Alamo engenders in sons and daughters native to the Lone Star State. Many connotations ride well the easy rhythm of this word's three rolling syllables, each bearing a weighty, unspoken obligation. In the wake of this word, mandates rise to the surface like night crawlers after a downpour. Those syllables also form the sacred cultural symbols that shepherd every Texas patriot's thoughts toward the trinity of duty, honor, and courage.

Nowhere in this same culture's lexicon is to be found the word *surrender*. We Texans are taught from the time we can toddle about and make sense out of language that *quit* and *surrender* are synonymous and not an option any real Texan would ever entertain. Our forefathers did not surrender at the Alamo, and, therefore, we are not about to quit anything we start or surrender to anyone, not even to God.

In the culture that raised me, Sarah, and you, too, almost every possibility of surrender is superseded by a strong commitment to winning. And this one belief, more than any other, has proved our greatest obstacle to living this life in the way our Creator intended.

We usually don't know this, of course, and that's why decade after decade we remain so tense, so driven, so worried, so attached to things, so obsessed with the illusions and symbols of success, and choose to live so close to the abyss that is exhaustion. We have been taught to accept as truth the culturally sanctioned conviction that life is only about winning, that quitters never win and winners never quit, when nothing could be farther from the truth.

The curious irony in all of this is that we cannot begin to know God and to follow Jesus until we surrender, but we will not surrender until we have absolutely no alternative. For that to happen, life must first break us open like a paper shell pecan. This is why for the vast majority of us, the idea of God remains a mere intellectual construct for the first half of our lives. Sooner or later, though, all of us discover that we cannot keep on winning—if we ever get to win—and simultaneously find the joy for which we so yearn. The truly happy among us are those few who have experienced the blessed, painful privilege that is all-out defeat.

I am one of those lucky ones, Sarah, because I have tasted defeat, and the experience hurt worse than I have the words to describe. Suffice it to say that I surrendered only because I had no other good choice. I was not wise enough to know that this course of giving everything, even you, to God placed my wayward feet on a path that has over time brought me great joy. I never really thought joy would, or even could, happen to me. But in the wake of my daily surrender, it has come upon me like a gentle autumn rain. And as long as I continue to give up the culturally conditioned habit of winning, joy follows me like a loyal old dog.

So my prayer for you, my daughter, is that when your life shatters like a pickle jar hitting a tile floor, you will know what to do—drop to your knees and speak these two words: "I surrender." From that point on, you will know what it means to have life and have it abundantly. I promise.

—Dad

Liberation

Dear Sarah,

To be sure, in childhood, our healthy development is contingent upon other human beings loving us. But once we become adults, we must swap this need for a new and often frightening dependence upon God. This is never easy, but if we are to be healthy, this is a shift that must occur. Once we make this shift, there can be no turning back. If we fail to make it, we never grow up, but spend our lives searching for people to liberate us from loneliness and the close-to-inconsolable despair that attends self-loathing.

When we are children, our parents are our gods. If they love us and liberate us, we step on the path that over the years can lead to spiritual maturity. If, however, they fail to love us, we have a good chance of growing up confused about everything, most especially about what it means to express love.

Mr. Dodd's barbershop was an institution in post–Second World War Dallas. It was a "manly" place filled with braggadocio and usually brimming with bluster about the war my father and his buddies had just won. Every possible shade of hair covered the floor until a black man, who owned no rights and who got little respect from the customers, swept it up once in the morning and then again in the afternoon. When he was not sweeping, he polished and buffed the shoes of men who tossed him a quarter when he was done. Through everything, he remained as silent as a stump and as obsequious as timidity itself.

Mr. Dodd finished with me first that warm morning, and I jumped down from his big leather chair with the crank on the side and reached inside my pocket. An hour earlier, my mother had given me two quarters, and I placed both in Mr. Dodd's palm. He received them and pushed a button causing the drawer of his cash register to fly open with a loud ring. After dropping the quarters in a tray, he brushed me vigorously with a talcum powder–soaked brush before offering me a neatly wrapped piece of bubblegum.

As I unwrapped it, I heard him say to my brother, "Okay, Billy Boy, your turn." Bill dropped his comic book and climbed into the chair I'd moments ago vacated. Mr. Dodd switched on the clippers, and I wandered outside to investigate the small world separating the barbershop's front window from the curb of Edgefield Boulevard. Soon enough, I discovered a pipe sticking out of the sidewalk, and, for no good reason, I rammed my arm into its inner recesses all the way to the elbow. To my shock, the thing struck back by "squeezing" my arm like a boa constrictor. I was hopelessly stuck.

I screamed for help, but no one in the barbershop could hear me because of the roar of the evaporative cooler that pumped water-cooled air inside. I cried, but to no avail. A fat, shirtless man running with small rivers of sweat and wearing a pair of baggy pants supported by suspenders happened by and said, "I know one little boy who just might lose his arm." Following this terrifying proclamation, he stepped into the barbershop and apparently reported my dilemma. Bill jumped out of the big chair and raced past me without a word on his way home.

Soon a crowd gathered, and each person in it offered at least one surefire strategy for liberation. Most involved cutting the pipe and then hauling me in an ambulance to a hospital.

I heard Bill's panting before I spotted his beautiful, grimy face. I knew that he'd run all the way home to inform my mother, who, no doubt, immediately called my father. As the crowd grew thicker and precariously close to acting on a plan, I heard my father's voice. I looked up and made out his handsome features through my tears. "Daddy," I said in much the way Jesus must have whispered that word in his language only hours prior to his crucifixion.

My father spoke not a word but gripped my arm firmly and yanked. My skinny arm popped out of that pipe like a wine cork. Pleased, he said, "Now let's go home." And the three of us climbed into the only car our family owned, me with one tingling arm, Bill with a half-cropped head of hair, and my father wearing a smile that signaled the mysterious, wonderful truth that love is liberation

I tell you this story, Sarah, to show you that love always liberates. I bumped into this truth somewhere during my fifth year of life, but, of course, I didn't embrace its meaning until decades later, when the circumstances of adult life compelled me to remember my first experience with the liberating power of love. Too often we erroneously equate love with some expression of neurotic dependency, which is synonymous with control. Love is not sick dependency. Love is liberation and also safety and freedom and so much more, but it is never grounded in the unhealthy conviction that our happiness depends upon another person's loving us when we're adults.

—Dad

Trapped by Circumstances

Dear Sarah,

LONG BEFORE MY BIRTH, AND ONLY ON ACCOUNT OF MEANNESS, someone deposited a yearling catfish into Uncle Will's pasture well. Actually, this well was nothing more than a hole half-filled with cold spring water. If our family dropped a bucket into it at all, it was only to water the hogs during a summer drought or to rinse the lint off our sweaty backs following a mercilessly hot afternoon in the cotton patch.

Every time I approached that well, I remembered the tale of the catfish. Further, I recalled hearing from my Uncle Carl and my dad that many times over the years, with the aid of a lantern, that poor creature had been spotted at night as he rose to the surface in search of some hapless grub or grasshopper that might have made the fatal error of tumbling into his watery domain.

The reports of this catfish were likely exaggerated, but consistently grotesque. I was told that his tail resembled the wiggling end of a pollywog, while his head had grown to the width of a grubbing hoe. Circumstances engineered by cruelty proved a source of anguish to me. In fact, sometimes as I lay in bed at night, I would pray for that fish to be set free because I was old enough to know that a catfish belongs in a creek, lake, or river, but never in a well.

This fish was trapped by circumstances beyond his control—helpless. But because Jesus has taught us how to pray, we, unlike that fish, are never helpless. Nevertheless, we still often find ourselves trapped in fear. Our fear can be transcended once we know to pray because courage is not the conquering of fear, but, rather, the delectable fruit of surrender.

Fear has a way of turning the reality of plenty into frightening images of scarcity. But in the wake of soulful prayer, our eyes are finally opened and we awaken from years of sleepwalking to discover two amazing truths: (1) we are free, and (2) grace is always sufficient. Once we make these truths our own, the strangest thing happens to our perception. Suddenly, scarcity becomes abundance, and all the toys we once thought would bring us the happiness we so long for lose their luster. And by the time joy finds us, much has changed—everything has become nothing and, believe it or not, nothing has turned into everything.

—Dad

Being Perfect

Dear Sarah,

THESE WORDS ARE CONTAINED IN CHAPTER 5, VERSE 48 OF MATTHEW'S Gospel: "Be perfect, therefore, as your heavenly Father is perfect."

I know of no words in the Bible more subject to misinterpretation in the cause of emotional abuse than these. Somewhere in childhood, most of us embrace as truth the insidious and destructive lie that we don't measure up and are, therefore, unlovable. For years we unconsciously attempt to counter this falsehood by living up to some rigid, homemade definition of perfection. Nothing could cause greater emotional, psychological, and spiritual damage.

Some years ago, I was invited to teach a class before about three hundred apparently prosperous young adults in a church located in one of Austin's upscale neighborhoods. As always, I was a bit uptight before addressing these people. As a young woman introduced me in terms that outstripped any semblance of reality, I fidgeted with a plastic cup half filled with tepid decaffeinated coffee. When it came time for me to approach the dais, I fumbled the cup and spilled coffee all over my pressed khaki trousers and discovered that decaffeinated coffee stains every bit as much as its more powerful cousin.

Here I was preparing myself mentally and emotionally to stand before a large crowd of up-and-in folks for about an hour. As I studied the dark, wet mess making a puddle in my lap, I realized that Jean-Paul Sartre was right—sometimes there is no exit. That morning, there was no escape from humiliation. In a moment when I sought to be my most impressive, my most "perfect," I appeared to have urinated in my pants.

I did the only thing I could. I tossed my notes aside and strode, as confidently as wet pants will permit, to that lectern in what felt like I was being washed away by a tsunami of ridicule, snickers, giggles, knowing glances, and nudges. Once there, I offered the following opening remarks:

It is very good to be with you this morning, even though it appears that I have wet my pants. Just as I let the cup of coffee slip out of my hand, I gave serious consideration to running out of here and never showing my face on this campus again. But that would not be right. What is always right is the truth, and, therefore, I decided to stay and tell you that I spilled my coffee in my lap because the idea of speaking before crowds terrifies me. I was once very ashamed of what the clinicians term a "social phobia," which is fear of public speaking, or, more accurately a deep-seated fear of humiliation. I'm very close to feeling humiliated right now. But it's okay if you laughed, snickered, or nudged the person next to you. I would have done the same thing had I been you. But in light of what I have done to myself in your presence, I've decided to speak today extemporaneously on the power of love to overcome the shame we attach to our imperfections. Your pastor invited me to speak on family communications theories, but somehow I don't feel right doing that with my pants all wet. Perhaps you can invite me back and I will gladly offer you the talk I had prepared for today. But this morning, I need to tell you about the power inherent in grace to overcome what shame might be attached to a grown man with wet pants standing before good-hearted people. And perhaps by the time I'm finished, you will have received a little help and my pants will be dry.

An hour later those folks assured me that the talk I delivered was as helpful as it was memorable. Never before have I seen people so interested in what I had to say, and seldom have I felt so at ease before anyone, once I told them the truth of my imperfection and the good news of God's unconditional acceptance of all of us mistake-makers.

What Jesus is declaring in his admonition in Matthew's Gospel has nothing to do with the ubiquitous heresy of "perfectionism"; it has everything to do with being patient with ourselves as we place our feet on the winding path toward wholeness. What Matthew is pointing to is the spiritual condition of wholeness, in which there are no deficits only because God is whole and, therefore, lacks in nothing.

Wholeness, then, is a description of the journey, not the goal. This idea is so difficult for us to understand that it often proves a stumbling block to us becoming who God made us to be. We are so conditioned by the threat of a shame attack that we seek to demonstrate a perfection that we believe perhaps might garner for us some small bit of praise. But in doing this, we fail to realize one very important truth: absolute Perfection has accepted our imperfections from the beginning. It is when we realize this gift and decide to embrace that acceptance as truth that we step for the first time on the path that leads us toward wholeness.

One step on this path is worth more than a million on any other, but even here our goal is not perfection, but, rather, the recognition that all of our imperfections have been accepted all along. Awareness is the seed of wholeness, and more than any other therapeutic strategy, this new insight possesses the power to liberate us from the habit of shame.

—*Dad*

November

Dear Sarah,

THE ARTIST SLIPPED IN LAST NIGHT, BENEATH THE FIRST FULL Halloween moon since your bed was a crib. I awoke to listen for her arrival, which was a waste of time because most often she insists upon silence. I remember, though, one Arkansas night only a few weeks before your birth when a fanfare of thunder seemed to shake the Ozarks before it rolled all the way across the river and into Tennessee. But that was a long time ago, and last night, November arrived to paint the Texas Hill Country with shades of crimson and orange and to join everything that has gone before, including the terror of September 11, with the whimper of a newborn.

I admire November for her humility and purposeful diligence. She is John the Baptist without the passion, bluster, and single-minded ravings of a man on fire with the truth. Subtlety is more her style, her message remains the advent of love, and her conclusion is the muted explosion of autumnal majesty. Most often, she departs as quietly as she arrived, leaving us grateful for her generosity and in awe of her handiwork. Sometimes I hear her sigh in a cool breeze as she carpets the ground with leaves only days before turned brilliant, and in those moments my heart is sad and yet rife with hope as I lean toward that place in my soul in which a new expression of love is waiting to be born.

—Dad

Patience

Dear Sarah,

THE APOSTLE Paul CAME CLOSER TO THE TRUTH, I SUSPECT, THAN any other human being ever has in describing, but not defining, the mystery that is love. In his First Letter to the Church at Corinth, he penned these immortal words:

> If I speak in the tongues of mortals and of angels, but do not have love, I am a noisy gong or a clanging cymbal. And if I have prophetic powers, and understand all mysteries and all knowledge, and if I have all faith, so as to remove mountains, but do not have love, I am nothing. If I give away all my possessions, and if I hand over my body so that I may boast, but do not have love, I gain nothing.
> Love is patient; love is kind; love is not envious or boastful or arrogant or rude. It does not insist on its own way; it is not irritable or resentful; it does not rejoice in wrongdoing, but rejoices in the truth. It bears all things, believes all things, hopes all things, endures all things.
> Love never ends. (1 Corinthians 13:1-8*a*)

As I read these words, I sometimes wonder if Paul intended a certain hierarchy in this description. For example, did he place the word *patience* ahead of the idea of being kind because it is more important to be patient than to demonstrate kindness? I doubt that any such arrangement was intended, and most likely he meant for every point to carry equal weight.

Be that as it may, I suspect that patience forms the foundation for all that follows in Paul's letter—how he describes love and, even more important, how he says we should experience this ever-mysterious love. If we do not choose patience, we cannot possibly be kind, and we will likely become controlling and, therefore, lacking in any real joy. Patience, then, is the first necessary step in experiencing the palpable, yet still ineffable, mystery that is love.

What, then, is patience? To begin with, it is not some warm feeling we conjure up, nor is it a divine gift that falls out of heaven like the acorn Chicken Little scared herself into believing was the sky. No, patience is the fruit of a well-honed discipline born only of wisdom. Every human being who is patient is this way because he or she has decided that patience is the wisest approach to life's daily challenges.

How did these patient folks learn this lesson? I suspect they learned it the same way we all discover any great truth— through the gift that is suffering, or what Jesus called being "poor in spirit." Where they once reacted reflexively, they now respond thoughtfully. Where for years they champed at the bit like a Kentucky thoroughbred in a starting gate, they now wait and even relax as they savor the moment.

Goodness and mercy trail behind those who are patient like two faithful old dogs as they take life one day at a time. To a person, the patient ones in our midst would choose kindness ten times out of ten over hurting another human being, no matter how seemingly beneficial the payoff. The patient know God; the rest of us wish we knew how to be patient and, even more important, how to know God. Blessed are patient people for, like God, they are expressions of love.

—Dad

Whitnee

Dear Sarah,

SHE ARRIVED IN THIS WORLD ONLY ELEVEN MONTHS AGO, AND THIS morning she came to "school," a child development center, for the first time. Her father stood on the sidewalk next to his open office door as I stepped out of my truck into the early November morning. I heard his familiar voice: "Hey, Bob, you wanna see someone very special?" I answered, "Sure." As I stepped into his office, I spied baby Whitnee, already the survivor of one major heart surgery.

Some would claim Whitnee is disadvantaged by the limits imposed upon her by Down syndrome. If we view her through the lens of the ego, we might regard her as unfortunate. But if we dare to stretch ourselves and look at her as God does, there is in her no disadvantage, nor does she have limits.

This is not some Pollyanna perspective, nor is it the expression of denial. In the world of the ego, in which competition is the route to our conclusions regarding self-worth, this little girl is, indeed, disadvantaged and limited. The reason seems obvious—she will not be able to "compete" with so-called normal children in games and academics. But when it comes to expressing love, Whitnee was born a true champion. Whitnee simply loves, and for the years God gives her to live, love will be her work, her mission, and her identity. Love knows nothing about competing or even about winning, unless everyone wins.

If anyone is to be pitied, it is the rest of us, for even at eleven months of age, Whitnee knows why she is here. The rest of us will spend most of our lives competing, clawing, and fighting our way to the top until, if we are fortunate, we come to realize that the only reality in this life is love. Everything else is an illusion. Whitnee already harbors this sacred truth within her soul while the rest of us invest our energy in struggling to discover our purpose. What a gift she is to her parents and to all who are privileged to catch a glimpse of her beauty, especially her toothless yet persuasive smile and her tap-dancing eyes.

—Dad

Rejection

Dear Sarah,

I WAILED IN AGONY AND CRIED LIKE I HAVEN'T DONE SINCE UNCLE Will's funeral. But on that memorable Wednesday in February, the telephone brought word of a different kind of death—the death of a dream. Even more, this call told of the demise of my attachment to my personal reason for being and proclaimed the end of an arduous, action-packed two decades' worth of self-absorption, self-defeat, and unholy obsessions. What I had made my personal deity was taken from me by a decision far beyond anything I could control, much less influence. The job I had always wanted would never be mine.

I was shocked. For days I walked about in a trance of denial supported only by a burgeoning sense of desperation that in time would turn slowly into a costly depression. Everything I imagined I'd ever lived for was yanked from me in this one decision. I despised those who had done this. For months, the atmosphere around me remained heavy with the pungent toxin of rage. And during the whole of this ordeal, pain became my constant (and despised) companion.

I hated. In fact, I hated with such fierceness that at times what boiled inside me frightened me. I walked up and down sidewalks on my daily breaks in the spring of that year and raised my fist toward the sky, as though I imagined God resided beyond the clouds. With each wave skyward, I railed.

I'd like to report that one day I suddenly changed, or that I bumped into some wonderful insight from which I drew a major "Aha!" But none of those phenomena occurred. Perhaps such transforming experiences happen for others, but they have never been the way God has worked with me. I've come to believe that this slow coming of awareness in my life has far more to do with my trenchant defenses than with God's way of doing anything.

Before I could begin to see the gift in this rejection—and there is always a gift in such painful moments—I had first to experience years of pain and self-inflicted suffering. God was patient with me because love is patient. Over the course of the next decade, I began to realize that my great suffering was the result not of being rejected, but of erroneous thinking. In short, my perspective on just about everything stank.

This personal heresy may be summed up in the following three points:

1. I unconsciously equated my personal agenda with God's holy will.
2. I made myself the object of my worship.
3. I refused to trust anyone or embrace as truth anything except my own faulty conclusions.

If my life had worked out as I always dreamed it would, my dangerous errors would have been sealed in my soul as truth. Thank God that never happened. What did happen was that my theological applecart was turned upside down, and I was left with the gift of time and with new prayers as tools to make sense of disappointment. The pain I had lived with became the most effective teacher I would ever know.

Rejection delivered me to where I am today. I have swapped heresy for three new truths:

1. This life is not about me; it is only about the expression of authentic love.
2. The Mystery I call God is in charge of my life. I must only show up and then get out of the way, but both of these are spiritual disciplines that are far more challenging than they appear at first glance.
3. I have no career or ministry or any other profession. My

life is my work, and my life work is to love God, other human beings, and myself with devotion to the truth.

Getting to the place where these beliefs became guiding truths was not easy. But that devastating rejection was both the impetus for growth and the greatest spiritual blessing I've ever experienced. The pain certainly didn't feel like much of a gift the afternoon I was told that my dream (along with my theological system) had died. Every time I experience rejection now, though, I no longer flinch, much less hide in anger. Rejection still hurts almost as much as it did the day I wrote the obituary for my dream. But when it comes, I have learned to remain still long enough to experience the awful feelings that attend such moments and then I offer this question to God: "Okay, Lord, what would you have me learn from this?" And, once more, in time, the gift arrives in the form of some new lesson that teaches me how to express love.

—Dad

Doubt

Dear Sarah,

WHEN I WAS A KID, UNCLE WILL WOULD BUILD TOMATO FRAMES
each winter. These rectangular frames were about the size of
a screen door. When Christmas was but a fresh memory, and
January turned the air cold enough to freeze the stock tanks
and bless the hog pasture with its finest dusting of snow,
Uncle Will could be found in the barn repairing last season's
frames and constructing new ones.

Over each wooden frame, he stretched a thin cloth as tight
as a drumhead. By Valentine's Day, he had turned the ground
beneath a large pecan tree with a spade and planted hundreds
of tiny tomato shoots. Each shoot was no bigger than a quarter standing on edge.

This "chore," as he called it, required more than a week, but
by the time March arrived, he had the tiny tomato shoots rooted.
If the radio broadcast from Rusk prophesied a freeze, he lov-
ingly covered those fragile shoots with the frames. By Easter,
the frames were stored for another season and the ankle-high
shoots were transplanted into his tomato patch, which was
located at the foot of the sand hill. And by early June, his
efforts joined with God's grace to produce tomatoes the size of
small pumpkins, which he sold in town for a buck and a quarter a bushel. It was a hard way to scratch out a living, but it
was Uncle Will's way, and it was noble work.

Years later, I have borrowed from the image of Uncle Will's
tomato frames in considering the issues of doubt and faith. From
the symbol of this man's life work, I have decided that doubt is a
good thing, in fact, even a necessary thing, because, like the

tomato frames, it protects the fragile bud of faith from winter's bite.

Sarah, you might think a freeze would be a more suitable symbol for doubt, but I disagree. For me, the fertile soil is God, and what springs from that loam is the bud of faith. At birth, every human being is born with the innate capacity for faith. But because the world is interested in expressing only a self-serving agenda, it attacks our link to the Transcendent. Our reaction is to develop a self-protective belief system, otherwise known as doubt. And as Uncle Will's tomato frames long ago protected tiny tomato shoots, we defend our hidden buds of faith with a perceptual frame of doubt.

The process of doubt's defending faith is so remarkable and so necessary to personal spiritual development that only God could have thought it up. Many Christians erroneously believe that questioning is bad or, even worse, that they should feel ashamed when they doubt. The opposite is the truth. Doubt is invariably a divine gift because doubt protects every fragile bud of faith until life turns sour enough for us to drop to our knees and ask for help. And it is in such moments that the protective frame of doubt is finally lifted, the homemade self, with all of its self-interested convictions, begins to die, and new shoots of faith grow.

When people in the church and beyond tell me that they doubt, I say, "Congratulations!" But when someone shares that she's never harbored so much as one doubt, I say, "Oh, I'm so sorry to hear that." Both the doubters and the cocksure Christians are surprised by my response. That's okay with me because as a pastor it is not my role to please them; it is my responsibility to share with them what for me has become the truth.

—Dad

Loneliness

Dear Sarah,

LONELINESS TORE AT ME THAT MORNING LIKE SOME WILD ANIMAL AS I sat beneath what scant shade a half-dead hackberry provided. In that moment back in September of 1968, I was a hundred miles from the young woman who would later become my wife and your mother. And I was one of sixteen Anglo students at an otherwise all-black university.

As I leaned my back against the rough bark of a tree not created for obliging accommodation, I watched through tears as other students celebrated one another's company. No one accepted me except the professors who taught me during that dreadful year.

The government had given me two choices: Do battle with ignorance in President Lyndon Johnson's "War on Poverty" campaign, or enter into combat in Southeast Asia. I was not spiritually mature enough to declare myself a conscientious objector, although I did certainly object to this seemingly endless conflagration. If I was anything at all, I was a depressed young agnostic who wanted nothing more than to attend graduate school, marry my childhood sweetheart, and get on with life by becoming the best teacher possible. But here I was stranded in a "foreign land," surrounded by people of dark skin, and, in the main, ignored while I trained to teach who the government called "the children of poverty."

I tried in vain to make friends, but the color of my skin worked against me. It didn't take long for me to realize that the other students had been so scorned by whites that they would find it difficult, perhaps even impossible, to entrust to me the precious gift of friendship.

The night before, I had attended a movie in the university's field house. The place was packed, and, to my chagrin, the feature film was *In the Heat of the Night*. The story is that of a black detective outsmarting a whole Mississippi town filled with every imaginable stereotype of white bigotry. When the movie was finished, I was bumped and jostled by several angry black youth who seemed intent on scaring me as I made my way to the exit. From out of nowhere, a white Catholic priest appeared, slung his arm about my shoulder, and said, "You look like you could use a friend." I don't think I've ever been so glad to see anyone. This man walked me to my car, where he bid me a solemn good night. I tried to thank him, but he disappeared before I could find the words.

Many times since that long season of isolation and fear, I have experienced a painful loneliness. Most often, this tangle of emotions and thoughts is the result of my decision to visit another kind of "foreign land." This inhospitable, but often strangely attractive, place is located in a desert where Jesus' words, "Thy will be done," hold little appeal. I have discovered that a dedication to promoting and defending myself can be the loneliest of all occupations.

So why do I visit there so regularly? The answer is as simple as it is sobering: I'm a human being.

—*Dad*

Ambivalence

Dear Sarah,

THE FIRST LECTURE I ATTENDED IN MY PASTORAL COUNSELING residency was offered by a psychiatric social worker. The course was entitled "Marital Therapy," and prior to launching into her introductory lecture, this woman asked that all pastors raise their hands. About half of us in that class of fifteen students complied. In response, she smiled knowingly and said, "You folks and morticians are the only professionals who work with people who are absolute, because when you officiate at a funeral, the body you say words over is absolutely dead. But in this life, the whole of humanity is always ambivalent."

I remember nothing else about that lecture, or even much about the course, but that at-first seemingly insignificant insight became an idea that would later hold great meaning for me. In fact, I today view this small bit of awareness as one of the most important lessons I learned in those two challenging years.

In my practice as a pastoral counselor, I have experienced many people who shame themselves or who even decide to destroy themselves with some virulent addiction or dangerous compulsion because, in their view, they cannot measure up to the unrealistic standards of absolutism. I've witnessed many clients fret and even experience panic attacks because they were not absolute about something or someone. Pastors have confessed that they are not absolute in their faith as they glanced from side to side, as though someone might hear and report their expressed doubts to the ecclesiastical police. Husbands have told me that they feel guilt because they've sometimes thought of leaving their marriages. Wives have told me much the same thing. Students have told me that they doubt that the career path they are choosing is really what they want to do with their lives. Often these students experience an almost debilitating depression because they have convinced themselves that they should not enter into some challenging field unless they are absolutely certain their choice is right.

Absolutism doesn't exist for us human beings until, as my former instructor suggested, we are dead. But for as long as we are alive, part of us will want to keep our commitments and, simultaneously, part of us will want out of our commitments. This condition is ambivalence, and this is an important part of what it means to be a human being. We all experience it all of the time. The healthy accept it and, at times, even enjoy it; the more anxious among us either reject it outright or accept it in some measure, but worry about it.

When people tell me that they are stuck in the unrealistic demands of being absolute, I often offer two admonitions, one of which is biblical and the other of which is homemade. The biblical is this: "Be still and know that I am God." And after you've come to remember the truth that only God can be God, permit yourself also to recall that every cultural expression of absolutism is an unobtainable myth, and that ambivalence is a big part of what it means to be alive.

—*Dad*

Grace

Dear Sarah,

IN THE BLUE-COLLAR, BACKWATER NEIGHBORHOOD THAT REARED ME, there were seven institutions we were taught never to question and always to revere: "Old Glory," the Holy Bible, motherhood, teachers, the church, the nuclear family, and Miss Mabel.

By the time I encountered Miss Mabel, reputation, rumor, and no small amount of exaggeration had elevated her to the rank of icon. She had begun her teaching career in the autumn of 1925, when the paint on the newly constructed Sunset High School in the Oak Cliff section of Dallas was still wet. In the summer of 1963, I was assigned to her senior honors English class by the first computer the Dallas Independent School District was to own.

In the first week of September, I shuffled sheepishly into her classroom to discover her standing behind a lectern with a scowl etched into what I suspected might once have been soft features. If the Almighty did in fact predestine people for specific tasks, it was obvious that this woman had been created by her Maker to scare the bejeebers out of us not-so-innocent youth in the cause of pouring a pinch of English literature into our heads.

I noticed two anomalies in this stark classroom. One, she'd brought with her a teacup-sized poodle that was the color of a well-toasted slice of salt-rising bread. Like her solemn mistress, this dog was also not about to put up with any nonsense. Two, there was a giant electric fan whose wire facing was rumored to have been pried off about the time of the Korean War and whose blades spun about as slowly as a wagon wheel on a steep grade. If there was any cool air at all flowing from that fan, I failed to feel it.

I eased cautiously into my desk and chose to say not a word. As Miss Mabel's dog scanned the room in search of any hint of mischief, this icon offered three equally discomforting pronouncements. First, she informed us that no one had ever dared to create in her classroom what she termed a "deportment problem."

Her second announcement concerned the fan. As though she were the president delivering the inaugural address, she paused for effect before announcing, "The fan will be switched off October 1. It will remain off until May 1. Is that understood?" We nodded in unison, even though everyone in that room, save, I suspect, the dog, knew that the temperature could linger in the high 90s or even the 100s through the entire month of October.

Finally she proclaimed, "Young ladies and young gentlemen, you will write for me your senior thesis. This paper will be the most important work you have yet produced. You will begin work on it the week before Thanksgiving, and it will be turned in to me, completed and winnowed of all errors, by the week before your graduation. In the past thirty-eight years I have given less than a dozen As, so don't get your hopes up. But if you strive toward perfection, you may achieve a grade of B, and that mark will be sufficient to exempt you from the final examination this spring. Is this clear?"

"Yes ma'am," we responded in unison, as though awe had mysteriously melded us into a Greek chorus. My buddy Tim, whom I'd known since second grade, kicked my ankle and whispered, "What the heck does 'exempt' mean?" The dog noticed this indiscretion and snarled.

Somehow I made it through that semester without suffering post-traumatic stress disorder, and, as much to my surprise as anyone's, I earned a B. True to her word, Miss Mabel had guided us to Thanksgiving and the beginning of our senior thesis, which she promised would remain in the vault of Sunset

High School until the Second Coming. Although I knew nothing at the time of apocalyptic theology, I found myself praying that Jesus might not tarry.

I chose to compare Daniel Defoe's two masterpieces, *A Journal of the Plague Year* and *Robinson Crusoe*. The idea came to me that Defoe wrote *Robinson Crusoe* as a hopeful and even wistful reaction to his dark chronicle of the bubonic plague's devastation of London. For the whole of the spring semester I wrote and revised seventeen pages so many times that by the final week I had convinced myself that I would never feel up to writing another word.

The turning in of our senior themes was a ceremony in Miss Mabel's class that in terms of splendor and reverence ranked up there with divine worship, funerals, and high school graduation. Row by row we stood and then shuffled forward in alphabetical order, passing in silence before the tense little dog.

The first morning of our final week, my friend Tim decided he had to know what made our class valedictorian so smart. As the dog rested on a plaid pillow in its tiny basket, Tim reached into the storage compartment beneath this brilliant young lady's desk and removed a brown paper bag. I turned to witness this small bit of larceny and froze as the little poodle silently elongated his neck so he might sniff the air for any hint of a crime. To my disbelief, I witnessed Tim extricating what appeared to be a mustard-soaked bologna sandwich from the bag. Tim tossed the sandwich to me across the aisle. I caught it over my shoulder like one of the countless footballs he had tossed in my direction during our decade of growing up together.

When panic strikes, my brain often flips the switch marked "judgment" to the "off" position. Consequently, I threw the sandwich away like it was some infectious lump of active bacteria. The bottom half of the thing slapped against the spinning blade of the fan that had been turned on on May 1. The sandwich sailed with the ease of a flying squirrel across the room, causing the little dog to do backflips as it barked in midair.

The sound of mustard-soaked bologna slapping the blackboard caused even the dog to cease. I squeezed my eyes tightly shut in the irrational hope that if I could not see Miss Mabel then, perhaps, she could not see me.

Her cold and controlled question crowbarred my eyes open: "Who did it?" Every face in that classroom, including Miss Mabel's and that of her tattling little mutt, was turned on me. I raised my hand and whispered, "I did."

Miss Mabel resembled a State Fair of Texas corn dog. From her teased gray hair to the tips of her high-top shoes, she was splattered with mustard. I was sufficiently conscious to realize that I had suddenly become the single student in the history of her distinguished career to embarrass her. I bowed my head as I heard her say in what was a restrained, but still terrifying, tone, "Young man, you go straight to Mr. Gwynn's office."

Mr. Gwynn was our beloved school principal, and, like me, a Presbyterian, although he was devout while I had no idea what that particular word meant. When I arrived in Mr. Gwynn's office, his secretary asked in surprise, "Why, Bob, what are you doing here?"

"I'm in big trouble."

"You?" she answered incredulously. "What in the world did you do?"

"I'd rather just tell Mr. Gwynn, if it's all the same to you."

Mr. Gwynn opened his office door and stepped into the reception area wearing his signature public relations grin. "Good morning, Bob," he said as he extended his hand. "What brings you to see me?"

"Mr. Gwynn, I threw a sandwich into the fan in Miss Mabel's room, and the thing blew up and flew all over that classroom, covering Miss Mabel from head to toe in yellow mustard."

Mr. Gwynn feigned a frown and said, "Well, son, I don't think that was very wise on your part."

Miss Mabel's voice pushed me into the principal's office like an unexpected storm-force gale. She and Mr. Gwynn followed. "Mr. Gywnn!" she barked as I trembled. "Bob Lively will not graduate with his class this week. He has failed senior English, and he will attend summer school. And, Mr. Lively, I care not in the least what this decision does with your plans for college or how this new arrangement might interfere with your former dream of a pleasant summer. For, young man, you will join me all summer in the very classroom which you moments ago contaminated with your monkeyshines."

She spun about and walked away. As I stared at Mr. Gywnn, he said, "Son, I can't get you out of this."

My attendance in Miss Mabel's class for the few days remaining in the semester was pro forma. I showed up because I'd yet to tell my parents I was not going to graduate with my class.

The day before the scheduled final, which I'd decided against taking, Miss Mabel returned our papers. She called each student's name, in alphabetical order, naturally. As my classmates filed forward, she handed each a manila folder with their thesis hidden inside.

The bell rang, but I still sat. I stood to make as unobtrusive a departure as possible and froze as Miss Mabel called my name. "Sit," she demanded. She walked quietly to the door like a preacher who had just finished a memorable sermon. The dog seemed pleased to know that I was on the verge of getting a much-deserved tongue-lashing.

"Go to my desk," she commanded. I rose and stepped dutifully toward her large desk.

"Take your paper from the folder."

With hands that could not stop trembling, I lifted the paper from its manila protector and through tear-filled eyes dared to read her critique. Beneath her near perfect handwriting was an unbelievable A–.

My heart thumped so hard inside my chest I could scarcely hear. But over the storm of mixed feelings vying for expression I did manage to hear Miss Mabel call my name one last time.

"Now, come to me," she ordered.

Again, I complied and drew near to her place at the door. I chose not to glance at the dog for clues.

"Young man, you have written an excellent paper. You will graduate with your class this Saturday night after all. You will even do so with honors. I never want to see you again, and I hope never even to hear of you again. Be that as it may, I will gift you with one last word before you leave my presence forever, for more than any student I've taught, you will need that word for the remainder of your life. And, Mr. Lively, that word is 'grace.' Go forward into your life and never, and I mean never, forget that word. Now, go and don't so much as look back or, like Lot's wife, you will very surely turn into a block of salt!"

And just as Miss Mabel had admonished, I did, indeed, go forward into this gift we call life and never did I forget either the word she gave me or the grace she so generously demonstrated on that spring morning so many years ago.

—Dad

Stockman's Warning

Dear Sarah,

A COLD FRONT BLEW IN LAST NIGHT TO DIVIDE AUTUMN FROM winter and to herald December's boisterous arrival. When you were a little girl, you and I annually rejoiced once the season of hot and miserable turned suddenly, bitingly cold. And I recall us celebrating for several reasons, not the least of which was the fact that we were warm while everything outside was frozen.

By working with the homeless during the years of your childhood, I became keenly aware of the suffering people endure when they have no shelter from the cold. I recall once when the temperature in Dallas plummeted to eight degrees. Every radio station in North Texas filled the airwaves with frightening prophecies in the form of what is called a stockman's warning. The local meteorologists were cautioning all ranchers to make certain that their livestock was protected from the cold. I found it ironic that not one station issued a "human being warning."

Without permission, Father Jerry Hill and I opened the church basement garage to serve as a shelter for our homeless brothers and sisters. I knew that if we asked the congregation if we could do this, they would say no. So we didn't ask, because if that congregation taught me anything, it was that it is far easier to get forgiveness than permission. In those days I had no worries whatsoever about losing my job, because for me to be dismissed as an associate pastor would have required a majority vote by the entire congregation. These people were by nature cautious, but most of them were good-hearted, and I knew they were not about to fire me for sheltering the desperate in the name of Jesus Christ.

As I stood at the window of my office that afternoon watching ice pellets bounce off the pavement below, I spied a pair of legs sticking out from beneath a parked truck. I grabbed my jacket and raced downstairs and out the church's side door to discover one of our soup kitchen regulars lying unconscious beneath the bumper of a parked pickup. This man was blind, and his white cane lay shattered at his side. At first, I thought him dead. I touched his neck to discover he was still warm, although I suspected that his extremities were in danger of frostbite. I covered him as best I could with my jacket and then turned around and hopped like a wallaby over the ice patches until I reached the church.

Inside, I called an ambulance and then returned immediately to this half-frozen man and waited for the EMS team to arrive. I heard the sirens almost immediately, and within minutes, four strong men lifted my blind friend onto a gurney. I asked one of them how long this man had likely lain beneath the truck. His answer bit into my soul more than even that day's icy breath. "Probably an hour," was his curt response.

As I watched the ambulance haul him away to the county's charity hospital, I wondered, as I have done countless times, why what Jesus taught is so difficult for us to embrace as truth. He never told us that we have to jump through hoops to follow him. To become his disciples, we don't have to be baptized, or take communion, or master the catechism, or believe any particular doctrine other than his Lordship. What he did tell us is that we must learn to see him in the sick who need our attention, in the naked who need our clothes, in the hungry who need our food, in the incarcerated who need us to show up in jails and prisons with a listening heart, and in the homeless who need us to welcome them into our homes and to share with them of our abundance.

That I risked offending the church for saving the homeless from winter's fury seems ironic to me today. But on that day long ago when I found a man, a child of God, lying near death beneath a truck, I failed to find much irony in our collective unwillingness to show hospitality.

—Dad

Perfect Timing

Dear Sarah,

I WATCHED WITH CURIOSITY AS THE RANCHER SLOWED HIS PICKUP TO a halt. I wondered where he might be hauling two rolls of half-green hay on a drizzly December afternoon that hid the sun and conspired with the wind to erode my resolve regarding all things spiritual.

This Hill Country rancher surprised me by punctuating his cautious slowdown with an abrupt U-turn, causing the trailer to swing behind him like it was an alligator's tail. He aimed his truck at a pasture on the opposite side of the two-lane black-top where six longhorn cows, one huge black bull, and a calf had interrupted their grazing to study the man and his maneuvers.

The bull was the first to react. His trot turned to a ponderous gallop, causing his expanse of horns to sway back and forth like oak limbs in a storm. The cows and calf followed. In no time, the bull was on the rampage, heading straight for the gate. It was then that I discovered the rancher's challenge. The man had to jump from the cab of his pickup, run toward the steel gate, swing the thing open, and rush back to his truck in time to drive into the opening, thus preventing the bull's escape.

By no more than a frog's hair, the man's timing proved perfect. His truck arrived just in time to interdict the bull's surprising progress. In fact, for a second I feared for this animal's well-being, as the truck appeared ready to ram him head-on. Although I estimated that the bull and the truck weighed about the same, I was prepared to wager the little change in my pocket on the truck. Just then the rancher hit the brakes.

He leaped again out of the cab and dashed to the gate, slamming the thing shut with one quick swing.

The bull disappeared behind the passenger side of the pickup. The rancher returned to the cab on the driver's side and began to roll immediately toward a gully. He soon disappeared from view with the longhorns trailing behind him.

I thought of God's timing and my nagging resistance to trusting anyone other than myself. Right there on the shoulder of that two-lane blacktop I decided that God must be much like this rancher. Heaven knows what we need even before we do, and even more amazing, God knows precisely when to open and when to close the gate.

Salvation

Dear Sarah,

A MAN CAME TO SEE ME THIS MORNING. AS HE SWAGGERED THROUGH the door of my office, he clung so tightly to the unexamined conviction that I might be able to help him that his knuckles assumed the color of snow. He began our conversation by telling me that I was the best at what I did. Such a comment points always to the same thing—a setup. Therefore, I allowed his accolade to slide off me quicker than churned butter sizzling a path across a skillet.

When I inquired as to what I might do for him, he groaned prior to asking me to fix him. "Fix you?" I responded incredulously. He laughed because he'd been with me before, and in making this request he recognized that he had pushed one of my buttons. "I can't fix you," I protested. The smile that spread itself across his broad face seemed to push against the forces of a lifetime of sadness and fear.

He vividly described his drug addiction, which, by the way, was the same issue he had brought to me almost a decade before. I decided the wisest course was to say nothing as he railed on about being sad, listless, anxious, obese, restless, and angry, among other complaints. I listened. Encouraged, I suppose, by my willingness to hear him out, he continued rambling on about one negative facet of his life after another. Finally, he sighed and declared, "My life is pure hell."

I thought it interesting that this man was quick to describe his life as torture while he seemed wholly unwilling to ponder even for a moment the possibility that it was far more likely that his existence upon this earth was intended by his Creator to be very much like heaven. Did not Jesus teach us to pray for a life "on earth as it is in heaven"? But to this confused man, heaven was to be viewed only as what awaited him when death finally permitted an escape from his current misery.

Like many people, this person was confused about what it means to be saved. Most likely, he long ago bought into the idea of salvation's having to do with being spared after death from a place of eternal punishment. What he didn't see was that, by using denial to defend himself against his present condition, he was disallowing his own salvation and simultaneously colluding with the part of him that would forever keep him unhappy.

Salvation is derived from the Latin word *salus,* which means healing. When we embrace this meaning, salvation becomes a reality every bit as important to the present tense as anything that might occur in the so-called hereafter. But before we experience this existential salvation, we must first become willing to collaborate with heaven by asking for help.

I could have told this man all of this, but I decided that any insight I might offer would make no real difference. So I sat in his presence for one painfully long hour as I prayed silently that someday he might discover the real meaning of what it means to be saved.

—*Dad*

First Communion

Dear Sarah,

I WAS MORE THAN MIDWAY THROUGH MY FOURTH YEAR OF LIFE WHEN my parents hauled me to the small county seat of Bonham, Texas, where I was to remain for four days in the care of my grandmother and grandfather while my mom and dad were off to Florida. They took my older brother with them, but I was judged much too active to fly halfway across the country.

I remember my mother's kissing me good-bye. Following that, my father took me in his strong arms as he offered what I recognized to be an uncommonly stern admonition. He said, "Now don't go messing with your grandmother, for she is one great lady." I wasn't sure what it meant to mess with my grandmother, and I was equally unclear about exactly what it meant to achieve the status of greatness. Nevertheless, I was certain of this one thing—if my father said my grandmother was great, she was something special because everybody I knew swore that my daddy was the most honest man they'd ever met.

The first day or so dragged by because there were no children in my grandparents' neighborhood with whom I might collaborate in the cause of adventure. Therefore, I busied myself by digging a hole in the side yard in search of something, but I don't remember what. Most likely, my hunt was for pirate treasure, even though Bonham is at least five hundred miles from any ocean. Perhaps my vivid imagination convinced me that some buccaneers had navigated up the Red River and decided upon my grandmother's yard as a good place to bury their purloined loot. After all, the Red River was only about ten miles away.

On the third day of my visit, I discovered a phenomenon—my grandmother's doorbell sounded exactly like her telephone. The implications of this arrangement proved too much of a temptation for my four-year-old curiosity. I could stand on the front porch of her prairie-style house, ring the doorbell, and then watch her answer the telephone with a pleasing Mississippi drawl. "Good mawnin'," she would say to the dial tone before I scampered away to hide in a hedge for the next several minutes.

On my fourth attempt at playing this trick on a woman my father had characterized as "great," I sensed an ominous shadow come upon me from behind as I pointed my small finger toward the doorbell. I whirled about to see my grandmother standing above me and smiling. Without a word, she picked me up and carried me into the living room, where she placed me in her lap as she sat in a rocker for what felt like an eternity. In spite of my promise not to mess with my grandmother, I had violated my father's edict. Consequently, I figured I deserved any punishment she chose to mete out, including a swift swat to my backside.

But no spanking arrived to bring me into line. This saintly woman only rocked and hummed what I would years later come to recognize as "The Battle Hymn of the Republic." After she decided that I had been calmed sufficiently by her soothing hymn, she lifted me again with what I expect was great effort, and carried me all the way to the kitchen. There she placed me on a wooden counter and raised her arms to a high shelf. She retrieved a large crock filled with more sugar cookies than I knew existed in the whole world. She walked to the icebox, from which she lifted a half-gallon jug of cold milk from a shelf. After filling a glass, she handed it to me along with two cookies and said something like, "Take, eat, this is for you."

In that moment, my grandmother taught me more about the true nature of God than anyone had in the first four years of life or, for that matter, has in the ensuing decades. Though filled with guilt and stung for the first time by that debilitating force we know as shame, my "punishment" was two sugar cookies and a glass filled to the top with cold milk.

From her small kitchen, this good woman then carried me to the rocker, where again she rocked as she hummed. All the while I munched on the cookies and washed them down with milk. When I was finished with the last bite followed by the final drop, she squeezed me gently and said, "Now, Bobby, don't go ringing my doorbell anymore." She had concluded her powerful witness to love with a version of the only admonition that ever belongs to grace: "Now, go and sin no more."

When in the opinion of the folks who governed the church I was old enough to take communion, I was invited for the first time to the Lord's Table. But what those in authority couldn't know was that I'd received my first communion from my grandmother five years before. On that unforgettable day, she served me the four-year-old's equivalent of wine and a communion wafer and introduced me to the power of grace to nip shame in the bud and to wash away all traces of guilt.

—Dad

Very Tired

Dear Sarah,

A WOMAN DRAGGED INTO MY OFFICE TODAY TO COMPLAIN OF BEING tired—close to being exhausted is more accurate. I listened because I recognized that this teary bit of insight was not her real problem, although she was convinced it was. Such is often the case with us human beings. We easily confuse the symptom with the problem, only to discover that when we treat the symptom, we are likely to exacerbate the problem.

I waited. With tears streaming down her cheeks, she reiterated, "I'm so very tired. I'm not doing my job well. My husband and I are on different schedules and seldom see each other, and I don't have the time I'd like to give to my children." I remained silent.

Finally, she quieted herself enough for me to offer the following: "Be still and know that I am God."

"What does that mean?" she asked.

"Well, for starters, it means you and I ain't God. The admonition is for both of us to be still and know something that we won't know and can't know until we make the decision for stillness."

"And what is that?"

"It is the truth that we are not God."

"How does that have anything to do with me feeling the way I do?"

"It has everything to do with your condition, I suspect."

"Tell me how."

"To begin with, only God can be God, and God is in the results business. This, then, is never our province. Our work is twofold regardless of what we do. We are, first, to show up and then, second, to get out of the way and allow the Spirit to work both in and through us. Being exhausted is a sign that we are not grounded in this simple stance."

"I don't understand," she cried.

"I didn't either for decades. But finally one day, after months of an exhaustion that was fast leading me into depression, it finally dawned on me that my problem was my flawed thinking. By believing that I was responsible for results, I was making myself sick. And once I came to understand and then embrace as truth the idea that this life is not about me but about love, something surprising happened."

"And what was that?" she asked.

"My exhaustion disappeared and my depression evaporated like dew on a July pasture."

"Why?" she asked.

"Because I finally took God's advice and decided that I needed to be very still every day for quite some time, I needed to allow myself to be vulnerable and authentic, and I needed to give the results and whatever glory might attend them wholly to God."

"Did it work?" she asked.

I smiled and remained very still as she slipped away with question marks in both eyes like the big block numbers that used to pop up in the country store cash registers of my childhood. Someday, I suspect, the truth will finally overtake her. Then she will know to give herself the gift of some much-needed rest. She will get very still, and for the first time in her life, perhaps, she will really know God.

—Dad

Belonging

Dear Sarah,

MY SECRETARY APPEARED UNEXPECTEDLY THAT MORNING IN THE soup kitchen located in the basement of Dallas's First Presbyterian Church. In a voice loud enough to carry over the din of chatter and complaints, she announced that the police were on the telephone asking to speak to me. I'd called the Dallas Police more times than I could remember, but this was the first time they'd ever called me. I handed my soup ladle to Big John Bell, the mentally challenged man I'd hired to serve as the dining room manager, and jogged to my office to take the call.

A male, no-nonsense voice on the other end posed this startling question: "Does a woman named Betty live with you, sir?" I hemmed and hawed before I said, "Well, sort of."

"Can we bring her to you? She's out here raising all kinds of hell at a truck stop on the Dallas/Mesquite city line and she claims that First Presbyterian Church is home. We can bring her to you, or we can take her to jail. It makes absolutely no difference to us. So which will it be?"

I answered, "Please bring her home, for she belongs to this body." Within a half hour, Betty was back in the soup kitchen, blaring out her seemingly endless repertoire of bawdy, off-key songs, all the while slapping men on the back as she worked this crowd of desperate, filthy humanity. I knew that before this day was done, she'd turn a trick or two on the church's front porch in exchange for a few swigs of Mad Dog.

Paul, the same apostle who banned women from church leadership, wrote these words to the ordinary men and women who comprised the small Christian congregation in ancient

Corinth: "You are the Body of Christ." This seemingly innocuous declaration has to be the most inspired idea ever to come through any man's mind. Think of what it means: ordinary people like you and me and even Betty comprise the physical body of the living God.

If people were to give that idea any thoughtful consideration, they'd either reject it outright or fall on their knees in reverential awe of the redemptive power of love and the radical nature of grace. Consider the implications. You and I and a woman most people would judge disgusting together comprise the earthly, postresurrection body of our Lord. And it is our responsibility to become conscious of being this body and then do what we can to hold it together until Jesus comes again.

This was the idea that came to me in the wake of the police officer's question. Whether we understand this belonging and whether we are judged respectable or despicable, all of us belong to Christ. So I welcomed Betty home on that memorable day, and, just as I predicted, she was drunk by sunset. She was dead by the end of that year. Nevertheless, throughout her tormented life, she always belonged to Christ, even if she wasn't aware of this amazing blessing.

—Dad

The Christmas of Your Birth

Dear Sarah,

TWENTY-EIGHT YEARS AGO TODAY, I DROVE IN A DOWNPOUR OF sleet on that snaky stretch of two-lane blacktop that joins Bald Knob, Arkansas, to Batesville. By the time I'd passed Velvet Ridge, the winter storm had abated enough for me to glimpse the distant lights of Denmark. I'd wasted the day in Little Rock, and I was ready to return home to our tiny rented house to await either the holiness of Christmas or your birth, whichever came first.

Although I was anxious to be off the slick highway, the lights of Denmark caused me to pull the Chevrolet to the gravel shoulder and step outside into the freezing night. I studied two distinct lights in the distance. One was a star glowing atop a small farmhouse; above it, on a mountain peak, blinked a red beacon warning low-flying aircraft of the presence of a tower. The first light was the symbol of love; the second signaled the place where a nuclear missile was buried and poised, ready to defend our national interests with unimaginably destructive power. As I shivered in the cold, I whispered a prayer beseeching the One who promised us that darkness would never overcome the light to make me a humble witness to the light.

The world into which you were to come at any minute was, and is, balanced oh so precariously between those two lights. Those lights reminded me that we have a choice: we can follow Jesus and choose peace; or we can wage war with God, with ourselves, and with our neighbors. God loves us so much that even the freedom to destroy ourselves is in our hands and also in our hearts and minds.

Since that bitter night, I've come to see that the small Christmas star on the farmhouse is far more powerful than the ominous light blinking atop the tower. I didn't come close to knowing this truth before your birth, Sarah, but, thank God, I do now.

—Dad

A Dallas Christmas Eve

Dear Sarah,

BY FAR THE MOST MEMORABLE CHRISTMAS EVE IN MY MEMORY WAS 1983. On November 18 of that year, we had opened the first ecumenical all-night shelter for the homeless in the history of Dallas. The story of this opening is long and fraught with detours and wrong turns, but on the first day of August that year, the mayor of Dallas called to ask me to help shelter the homeless.

In truth, this building wasn't much of a shelter. It consisted of a concrete floor, four walls, a ceiling that no longer leaked, and space heaters strong enough to warm this 33,000-square-foot warehouse even on the coldest night. Since the Dallas Mavericks' inaugural season, this old warehouse had housed the wooden basketball court on those nights when the home team was out of town. The mayor and an assistant city manager had found another storage place for the floor, and the Episcopal-Presbyterian Shelter, Inc., rented the warehouse-turned-shelter from the City of Dallas for one dollar a year.

The first week of December, one of the wealthiest women in the world called from New York to ask if I had any ideas regarding how she might show her stepchildren the real meaning of Christmas when they visited Dallas over the holidays. I invited her to meet me at my office on Christmas Eve at 8:00 P.M. and I would show her and her family, including her famous husband, a Christmas they would likely never forget.

They arrived at my office promptly at 8:00. I'd met these people before; and although I was most glad to see them again, we kept our greeting brief because the windchill that night had plummeted below zero. They followed me as I drove slowly through the empty streets of downtown Dallas. There was no one in sight.

As we stepped out of our vehicles to approach the Austin Street Shelter's front door, I sensed their anxiety. I said nothing to indicate exactly where I was taking them. The building was nondescript and uninteresting. I banged on the metal door like I was pleading for access to a Prohibition-era speakeasy, and I heard a gruff voice on the far side ask my identity. I screamed my name, and the door slowly swung open.

The temperature outside was eight degrees, but inside the big heaters had warmed the air to a pleasant seventy-two degrees. My guests followed close behind like so many baby geese. When I lifted my hat from my cold head, most in the crowd of homeless men and women recognized me and began calling to me. A young alcoholic woman whose street moniker was "Rebel" yelled this request: "Hey, Bob, say a prayer for us. After all, this is Christmas Eve!"

"What shall I pray?" I asked.

Rebel was quick to answer: "Please thank God for us that there is a place for all of us tonight to be safe and warm."

That was the thrust of the simple prayer I offered as I stood atop a metal folding chair. Almost before I could say amen, I heard a hoarse voice in the back of the warehouse singing the first words of "Silent Night." Soon the entire crowd of four hundred homeless men and women joined this voice in offering praise to God in the most off-key and yet the most beautiful hymn I'd ever heard.

I turned to see both the wealthy woman and her famous husband in tears, and I knew that in that moment they and I had, indeed, witnessed the true meaning of Christmas.

—Dad

Seeing Jesus

Dear Sarah,

BIG JOHN BELL, A THREE-HUNDRED-POUND SAINT, SERVED FOR ALMOST a decade with me as my soup kitchen manager. John was mentally challenged, and he never learned to read or write. When I first met him, he was living on the streets of Dallas eking out a living, if you could call carrying heavy loads for less than minimum wage a living. I suspect most every employer took advantage of John because he could not read, write, or count. He worked all day and accepted whatever "the man" paid him.

He was born with the sweetest spirit I've yet to meet in a human being. John was very close to pure in his expression of love, was always responsible, and could be trusted to show up on time every day and do exactly what was expected of him in the soup kitchen.

Father Jerry Hill and I trained John well. We taught him how to set up the tables in the same spot on the floor every day and how to slip ten folding metal chairs around each table. He was the picture of precision in accomplishing his tasks day in and day out. He never faltered in his duties or changed his routine. Thanks to John, the soup kitchen opened at the same time every day and closed promptly at one o'clock after feeding anywhere between three hundred and five hundred homeless men, women, and children. I am told that my successor at First Presbyterian Church gave John a brass nametag. John wore that inexpensive little piece of brass with such pride that a stranger might think the president himself had pinned the Congressional Medal of Honor on John's shirt pocket.

One morning not long after the New Year, a woman came to my office to cry more tears than I thought could flow from one human being. Her sobs were so deep they shook her small being. The night before, her husband of thirty something years had informed her that he no longer wanted to be married. With that announcement, he abandoned her to experience her shock alone. She could not sleep, and I found her waiting for me at the door of my office when I arrived at the church to open the soup kitchen.

All I knew to do in those days was to listen, which is seldom a poor choice. This woman cried herself through one box of tissues after another behind my closed office door. I figured that she needed to cry, vent, and then cry some more, and that compassion lay on the side of patience. So I listened to her cry and only moved so that I might retrieve a fresh box of tissues, which she used as quickly as she had the first.

I had instructed John never to bother me during the morning unless (1) a fight broke out in the soup kitchen dining room, or (2) someone became very ill. I heard a soft tapping on the closed door. I rose, thinking this had better be good, in fact, very good. In the doorway, grinning like a mule chewing cactus, stood Big John Bell. I asked with a certain edge to my tone, "John, what is it?"

His answer seems bizarre when I write it, but in the context of working in the soup kitchen I'd become accustomed to accepting the unexpected. He said, "Jesus is in the Stewpot." The Stewpot is what we called our soup kitchen.

"What?" I asked, not certain I was hearing him, as the brokenhearted woman continued to sob in the background.

With emphasis, Big John repeated, "Bob, Jesus is in the Stewpot!"

I said, "Well, John, don't worry about it. Last week we had Queen Victoria and not long ago we had Muhammad Ali."

John seemed upset with my cavalier response. "But, Bob," he argued, "I told him about you, and he said he wants to meet you."

Now impatient, I responded, "Big John, I don't have time for Jesus. Tell him I'll be out there at noon to say the grace before we serve the meal. I'll meet Jesus then."

John shrugged and turned away, obviously disappointed in my unwillingness to share his enthusiasm.

An hour or so later, I escorted the grieving woman to her car and dashed to the entrance of the soup kitchen, only to find John grinning once more. In a tone louder than the speaker at the Greyhound bus station down the street, he said, "There he is! There he is, Bob! Jesus sure as shooting done come to the Stewpot!"

Before me sat a silent man who appeared to be about thirty years in age, and he was dressed in a clean, light blue robe with immaculate white trim. His beard was neatly trimmed, his eyes dark brown, his facial features smooth but swarthy, and his slight smile seemingly genuine. In his right hand he held a wooden shepherd's crook.

None of the soup kitchen regulars would sit at the table with this man. The consequence of this distraction was that the number of people waiting to eat was greater than usual or necessary. "Here," I barked to the line of street characters as I pointed to the man in the robe, "come sit down. This gentleman is not going to hurt you." Cautiously, eight or nine men made their way to the table and took their seats.

John interrupted my attempts to get things under way with a question that proved strangely embarrassing to me. "Aren't you going to let Jesus say the prayer? After all, he's God."

"No," I barked. "I'm in charge of this soup kitchen. Let's bow our heads and pray." Before I closed my eyes, I noticed that this man, who resembled every Sunday school picture of Jesus I had ever seen, had bowed his head in silence.

Because we were short of volunteers, I ladled stew that noon. Table by table, the men came forward to pick up a bowl of hot stew and a generous slice of homemade cornbread. Most mumbled a humble thank-you as I placed the hot bowl into their callused hands.

For some reason, and I'm not sure why, I looked up in time to see the man dressed as a popular rendition of our Lord smile at me, more with his eyes than with his mouth. "Thank you, brother," was all he said as he took the bowl and received the cornbread. Shivers climbed up my spine like a thousand tiny spiders, and I paused long enough to watch him return to the table.

By the time I'd finished serving second and third helpings to the hungriest in that day's crowd, Father Jerry Hill had returned from a fund-raising effort. I responded to his greeting by nudging him and announcing with a definite tone of sarcasm in my voice, "Hey, Jerry, we have Jesus here with us in the Stewpot today." With that, I pointed to the man sitting alone once more at the table and smiling as he held his shepherd's crook and gazed at the two of us.

For as long as I live, I will never forget Jerry's question: "How do you know it's not?"

"I don't," I answered. "I don't."

We were never to see Jesus again in the Stewpot—at least not in this form.

—Dad

Silence

Dear Sarah,

UNCLE WILL, WHO COULD NEVER SEEM TO MANAGE TO FIND MUCH fault in his grandchildren, would say to me on occasion, "Bobby, you talk too much with your mouth."

As I grew into an adult, I came to learn the great value of silence. Again, I seldom practiced it because I was much too invested in being impressive and in becoming the next rising star in the church. Nevertheless, at some level I knew that there was immeasurable value in silence.

After I began to understand that true spirituality meant being dedicated to the truth, I discovered the healing properties of silence. I even began the practice of daily contemplative prayer. Initially, my efforts with this discipline proved difficult and frustrating. But in time, I actually began to "hear" holiness in the silence. After each mystical experience, I knew more about the wisdom of following the ancient psalmist's admonition to "be still and know that I am God."

Today my life works better than it ever has. I strongly believe this improvement can be attributed to replacing my habit of impulsive chatter with a new willingness to listen conscientiously to the silence. In fact, at every meeting I attend, whether it be a church staff meeting or a nonprofit board meeting, I write on a scrap of paper these words borrowed from an ancient Jewish proverb: "I've never had to repent for what I didn't say."

Prayer and the discipline of silence have helped me enormously. Since I've begun the regular practice of waiting before I say a word, I've been amazed at the wisdom I regularly express by saying absolutely nothing.

—Dad

Giving My Father a Hand

Dear Sarah,

MY EIGHTY-TWO-YEAR-OLD FATHER STUMBLED AND FELL ON Christmas night. As you recall, he was helping his other granddaughter, Debbie, carry a stack of boxes to her car. I should have helped her, but, being who he is, he insisted, and the consequence of his automatic kindness was that he ended up on the sidewalk. By the time I reached him, he was sitting up on the curb in front of his house. I was glad to see him sitting upright, but I was still worried. Only months earlier, he'd taken a tumble on the golf course and fractured his shoulder blade in at least twenty places.

I immediately sensed his humiliation. He's always been a proud, take-charge kind of man. He had to be strong and hearty to survive the Great Depression and the Second World War. I hated to have to pull him up because I knew it would only add to his embarrassment. I tried to reassure him with, "It happens to all of us." He didn't respond. I repeated my reassurances, and once more he ignored my futile attempt to universalize his dilemma.

I suspect he recognized that my attempt to reduce his discomfiture was as feeble as his legs had become. But he and I both knew the truth: although all of us do fall, when we're young, strong, and agile, we can easily right ourselves. When we're very young, or ill, or growing old, though, we sometimes cannot pull ourselves up, dust ourselves off, smile at the embarrassment of it all, and get on with life.

When I was a child, he picked me up more times than I can remember, and throughout the life we have shared, he has often carried me both physically and emotionally when I was too weak or too sick to carry myself. Once, when my younger brother, Johnny, stumbled and fell against a sharp rock on a Colorado mountain, I saw my father pick his young son up and run uphill until he reached the car. His quick action and strength saved my brother's life.

But this time he was the one who was down, and it was my job to pull him up and preserve as much of his dignity as possible. Returning him to his feet was easy, but convincing him that I thought no less of him because of his feebleness was not. I did my best, but I never sensed that he believed me. All the way back into the house, he kept explaining himself while I remained silent.

Throughout our lives, love is often demonstrated through what we believe is strength. This is not altogether erroneous; it is simply the way we know, both in the family and in the world, to express love. But as I lifted from the sidewalk a person who had invested his life in lifting and holding his family together, I recalled these words from the apostle Paul: "My [God's] power is made perfect in weakness" (2 Corinthians 12:9).

—Dad

Going Home

Dear Sarah,

ALBERT WAS LIKELY THE OLDEST MAN EVER TO STEP INTO OUR SOUP kitchen. Of course, I didn't know this for a fact or even that the scarecrow of a man who more dragged than walked into the front door of our basement dining room was named Albert or that he was even older than he appeared at first glance. When I first caught sight of this man, I wasn't even certain he was alive, except that he was upright. I joined Father Jerry Hill and Big John Bell in catching him before he toppled over into the flow of traffic on Jackson Street.

This old man was covered from head to the dirty bottoms of his holey shoes with what as a kid I called stinkbugs. His skeleton-thin frame was alive with black creatures about the size of small roaches, and they emitted a defensive odor when threatened. The consequence of our preventing this old man from being crushed beneath the wheels of Dallas traffic was that Big John, Father Hill, and I were also all covered with a repugnant stench.

I led this addled, reed-thin man into the soup kitchen's one shower and did my best to pull his filthy clothes from him as what appeared to be a million black, stinking insects made their getaway. Throughout the dining room, I could hear men swearing at those bugs. I was too preoccupied to give much thought to city health codes and such as I bathed the old man's trembling body with a frayed rag soaked in antiseptic soap and hot water.

At my instructions, Big John dried the man with a towel and dressed him in a donated suit that was not even close to fitting. When he finished, he brought this ancient traveler to the cubbyhole that served as my office. I motioned for him to be seated, and he gratefully followed this simple instruction. His trembling turned to sobs as he bowed his head.

"Who are you?" I asked.

His sobs provided no clues.

Once more I asked, this time leaning toward him.

"What is your name, sir?"

He continued to cry and shake his head from side to side as though his name were "no."

I noticed that he was attempting to hand me something. Cautiously, I reached toward him and opened my palm beneath his clinched fist. Slowly and with what appeared to be a great effort, he opened his fist, allowing a wad of paper no bigger than a gum wrapper to drop into my hand. He had held tight to this clue through everything, even the shower we had so rudely thrust upon him.

I opened the wad to read a faded phone number with what I recognized to be an out-of-state area code. I placed a call to the number in New York City only to hear a gruff voice answer.

I introduced myself, and the voice asked, "What the hell do you want, mister?"

Trying to remain unruffled, I did my best to explain that the old man now sitting across from me in a suit that all but swallowed him had given me this number.

Suddenly the gruffness turned into a kind of audible Roman candle as he fired questions at a faster pace than I could possibly answer. "What? Where? Who? When?" the voice fumed. Finally, he paused to catch a breath, allowing me to explain how it was that I happened to come into possession of his phone number.

Next his question was, "How much?"

By now I'd learned to wait with this voice. He must have asked me six times how much money I wanted to return the man, now sobbing, with his head bobbing about like it was attached to his shoulders with a spring.

"Sir, I don't want any money. This is not extortion. I am a pastor and this is a Presbyterian church in Dallas. We only want to get this man off the street. That's the reason for this morning's call."

Sounding relieved, the voice in New York put a woman on the phone. I was told she was my visitor's very worried sister. She explained that the old man, her brother, whose given name was Albert, had wandered away weeks before from a nursing facility in upstate New York. The police and even the FBI had searched for him to no avail.

Before the winter sun had time to set, I drove Albert to the Dallas–Fort Worth airport, where I deposited him at the ticket counter of a major carrier. After parking the car, I dashed into the terminal, praying to God that he had not wandered off again. But by grace and the kindness of a young lady behind the counter, Albert had stayed put.

I bought him a soda, and the two of us sat in the waiting area until his flight to New York was announced. When permission for boarding was finally granted, Albert refused to rise from the uncomfortable chair. As sobs threatened to consume him once more, he managed to mutter, "I'm scared. I've never been on an airplane before."

Time was definitely a factor; therefore, I realized that any attempt at persuasion must be as effective as it would need to be swift. I knelt before Albert like a supplicant in desperate need of forgiveness. He refused to look at me because I suspect he felt simultaneously bewildered and terrified.

"How about if I get on the plane with you?" I asked.

He nodded and attempted to stand. I draped his frail arm around my neck and walked under him, holding him as tight as though he were a comrade wounded in battle. For some reason, I glanced at his feet and noticed that he had stepped out of both shoes and was now more shuffling about in his sock feet than walking toward the plane. When I arrived at the place where a woman was collecting boarding passes, I explained the situation as efficiently as I could. The woman signaled someone, and suddenly the entire line of restless travelers stopped until Albert's shoes could be located.

This was the age of laxer security, and most anyone could board a plane. When I asked the woman at the boarding pass station if I might walk Albert to his seat, she smiled and nodded. As a hundred or so people waited behind us in various states and demonstrations of patience and impatience, I slowly supported this old man to his assigned seat near the front of the fuselage. As the other passengers boarded, I sat for a moment next to him and held tightly to his hand in silence.

Finally, Albert loosened his grip. Perhaps he felt safe or simply resigned to his fate. Whatever the reason, a quiet settled upon him like fine dust after a windstorm. I bade him goodbye and quickly exited the plane.

At the plate glass window, I watched the jet carrying old Albert take off and then disappear into Dallas's cold night sky. And in that moment, I recognized that Albert had become for me a symbol of the condition that is universal to us human beings: at some time in our lives, every one of us becomes lost, and about all that we know is that we must do whatever it takes to find our way home. Fortunately, that is all we need to know.

—Dad

What Really Counts

Dear Sarah,

IN HIS LETTER TO THE CHURCH AT GALATIA, PAUL WRITES, "THE only thing that counts is faith working through love" (Galatians 5:6). Uncle Will said it just about as well, I suspect, when he said to me one morning in the milking pen, "Every stool must have three legs."

Most of us get into trouble because we want to be religious, or have faith, when we have no more real experience with what it means to love than a cow knows calculus. I've so often seen this problem manifest itself in the church. For example, just yesterday I got a Christmas card from a man who claimed to love me.

Like me, he's a minister, and his credentials as a pastoral counselor are identical to mine. The last time I recall visiting with this pastor was six years ago, and even then, our sharing was cursory and strained, at best. Last summer I bumped into him again at a church meeting and prepared my greeting only to see him avert his eyes. He turned away for whatever reason, so I decided against imposing upon him. Of course, I never know why other people do what they do, but their behavior is seldom, if ever, about me. Consequently, I gave this man's obvious, though subtle, rebuff little thought until I received his Christmas card professing to love me.

I placed his card on a table and stared at the thing as I sat back and pondered his message. I wondered if he knew what it meant to love. Next I questioned whether he really loved me or whether he was attempting to manipulate me in the cause of providing his practice with counseling clients in the coming year. I was ashamed for harboring the idea, but in retrospect, I suspect it came to mind because in the past I would have been every bit as disingenuous in the hope of benefiting myself.

Since I've begun to make prayer the top priority in my life, I've learned this: faith without authentic—and that means costly—demonstrations of love is about as worthless as Confederate money. We can say what we like and profess whatever sounds noble, but until we make the expression of truth a daily discipline, we will have no real experience with love. Without this devotion to truth as a foundation, our faith will remain meaningless, and all expressions of affection and feigned devotion will sound as hollow as they are.

I tossed this man's Christmas card in the wastepaper basket, not because I was angry, but because his words hit much too close to my own temptation to be dishonest. Today I don't tell others that I love them unless I am willing (1) to tell the truth, no matter what, and (2) to stretch in the direction of their highest good, even if such a move causes me to make a quick exit out of their lives.

I made this decision because I've come to believe that love is synonymous with truth and is also the genesis of all real freedom. Any expression other than authentic love is a waste of time.

—Dad

Attending Church Meetings

Dear Sarah,

BEFORE YOU WERE OLD ENOUGH TO TURN EXPERIENCE INTO memories, I faithfully attended every regional ecclesiastical meeting. In the polity of the Presbyterian Church, these are called Presbytery meetings, which literally means "a gathering of elders." And, believe it or not, I was an "elder" at the tender age of twenty-six.

After three or four years of attempting to remain faithful to the idea I picked up in seminary that these meetings are important, I gradually reduced my attendance to once a year. When my record began to reflect a certain lack of interest, I became anxious and decided I would once again attend most of these meetings, but I would linger only a few minutes at each one and thus satisfy the requirement of having attended. This practice met the letter of church law but certainly not the intent of the attendance requirement for all ordained clergy.

The consequence of this practice is that if I'm thought about at all by the Presbytery that holds my membership, it is as somewhere between a pariah and a very poor churchman. I confess readily to the latter charge and will leave the first allegation to the judgment of those who find satisfaction in judging. The reason I no longer attend is that I've never found much more to those lengthy meetings than the systematic and always decorous expressions of the personal agendas of the ego. I sometimes wonder if the Holy Spirit ever bothers to show up, even though his name is invoked repeatedly.

If I have a favorite locale for these meetings, it is on the campus of Schreiner University in the Texas Hill Country. Each June the Presbytery meets in this institution's quaint auditorium. I arrive early, register, and then hurry to my pickup truck to avoid being spotted and turned in as the renegade I am. On my way home, I always stop in Fredericksburg, which, for a few weeks each summer, becomes one of the several unofficial "peach capitals" of our state. A five-dollar basket of freshly picked peaches seems to make bearable the ordeal that is Presbytery.

On one particular trek to the Hill Country, this one made in a rented Oldsmobile, I experienced a premonition that I would have a flat before I arrived at the meeting. I'm not in possession of any particular gift when it comes to clairvoyance; nevertheless, I knew that the well-abused car I was driving would blow a tire. I suspect that all of us know these things every so often. No one can explain how it is we know what is going to happen; we just do.

A mile or so west of Johnson City, I felt the right rear tire flapping beneath me like the broken wing on a wounded mallard. I carefully pulled the car to a stop and replaced the tire with a spare that was balder than even my smooth head. Feeling a bit insecure with this arrangement, I returned to a service station, where a kid who appeared young enough to look forward to his high school graduation greeted me with a wide grin. Within minutes, he repaired the tire while he regaled me with wild tales of how he and his grandpa caught trophy bass in a "secret" lake nearby.

When he was done, I tipped him even more than the cost of the repair. The kid grinned as I half joked, "I'll tell you what. If you will divulge to me the whereabouts of that 'secret' lake, I'll make it worth your while."

"Can't do it, Mister. I done swore to my grandpa I never would tell."

"I admire your integrity," I said through the Oldsmobile's half-open window as I backed out of the service bay.

I registered at the Presbytery meeting and returned immediately to the Oldsmobile to drive into Kerrville in search of some out-of-the-way place to enjoy a good lunch without being spotted.

I happened upon a tiny sandwich stand attached to another service station. Behind the counter stood a lovely young woman, about your age, Sarah. She had obviously been devastated by a stroke. The entire right side of her body appeared paralyzed, and her limp was not only noticeable, but also painful to see. I felt as though I were imposing upon her as I watched her write my order for a turkey sandwich. As she turned away with my order in her hand, I ached for her. I wondered what she might be doing instead of making me a sandwich had whatever force crippled her not won a cruel victory. The thought stung so, I abandoned it.

After I finished my sandwich, I paid her and, as with the kid who repaired my tire, I tipped her more than the amount of the check. As I drove away, I prayed that she would not view this spontaneous burst of generosity as an expression of pity. I was comforted by the idea of being powerless over what she thought. The tip felt right, and I was glad that I had offered it. My motives seemed clean enough.

A half an hour or so later, I pulled off the highway again, this time at a peach stand on the east side of Fredericksburg. As I entered the small open-air market, I spied another kid, this one about twelve years of age, who was engaged in weighing his head in a set of produce scales. I asked, "How much does your head weigh?" Twisting his neck in the attempt to read the scales, he answered, "About nineteen pounds, I reckon." We both laughed before I opined, "Well, you must be toting about one heavy load of brains."

This youngster sold me a basket full of peaches picked the day before, he told me, from his daddy's orchard. "Does your daddy know you weigh your head?" I asked. "Naw," he answered obviously embarrassed. As I turned to leave, he stunned me. "God bless you," he said.

I paused and then answered, "Well, I think God has done just that today—at least three times."

—Dad

Anger

Dear Sarah,

A WOMAN I ONCE BEFRIENDED SURREPTITIOUSLY ATTEMPTED TO eliminate my column in the *Austin American-Statesman*. As you know, I've been writing that column for more than a decade, and suddenly it was gone quicker than smoke in a high wind. You can imagine my astonishment in discovering that this woman, a person whose job I had once helped save, was a big player behind the decision all but to eliminate my voice in this community. Initially, I was deeply hurt; later, I was very angry.

I steamed for days. Out of the blue, she called to apologize. I view apologies as vacuous expressions of the ego. Every time we apologize, what we are really saying is this: "Please don't stay angry with me, because I am uncomfortable with your anger." Apologies, then, are often self-serving and seldom, if ever, promote healing, and this is because apologies refuse to accept full responsibility for the pain we inflict. Amends, though, are declarations of the willingness to assume full responsibility for the pain we cause. Consequently, only amends can begin the healing process when a relationship is torn asunder. The expression of an apology is to say, "I'm sorry," while an amend goes something like this: (1) I recognized that I injured you; (2) I regret that I injured you; (3) I injured you because I was not mindful of my responsibility to love, no matter what; and (4) I will not knowingly do this again.

Anger is not a bad thing; it just is. As I often tell clients, we are "wired" for anger, and it is only what we do with our anger that determines morality. If we act on it, we will almost always regret the decision. If we repress it and deny its existence, we will likely internalize it, with the result being the onset of a psychosomatic illness, perhaps even depression.

So what are we to do with anger? We must first feel it and permit its presence. I have learned to do this by telling myself, and God (as though God didn't already know), that I am very angry. Next, we must surrender it to God. This means give it up. This is never easy and takes years of practice buttressed by the discipline of prayer.

In truth, I wanted to retaliate against the woman who injured me. That's the ego's "solution," the old "eye-for-an-eye" ethic. But this never works. All retaliation does is create an emotional slugfest that no one wins. The only thing that works is what Jesus told us to do: pray earnestly and sincerely for our enemies.

The Bob in me wanted to inflict on this woman the same emotional pain she had caused me, but the Christ in me would have no part of that sick strategy. I find myself praying for this woman every day now. And in my prayer I ask God to bless her with her heart's desire. Every time I make this prayer, two ideas come to me. First, this woman is not my enemy, because when we pray for someone, he or she ceases to be the enemy. She may well consider me her enemy, but she is no longer an enemy as far as I am concerned. And second, this life is not about my being right; it is about my expressing love, especially when I believe that I have been wronged.

I've discovered the hard way that I cannot remain angry and operate within the boundaries of God's will. It's not that God is opposed to anger; it's that God's will is invariably the expression of love. Anger can be one very slippery slope and can cause us to slide far away from God's best intentions for us. Consequently, with all of the emotions I experience that make this life so interesting, anger is the one to which I must pay the closest attention. When I get angry, I must "feel the feeling" and then call upon the Spirit of Christ to take over. Left to my own feelings and clever rationalizations, I am a man who can injure others.

—Dad

Celebrating the New Year

Dear Sarah,

I'VE NEVER BEEN MUCH IN FAVOR OF CELEBRATING THE ARRIVAL OF the New Year. When I was a kid, December 31 never felt like anything new. When January finally arrived, I was in the same grade I'd been in the year before, and I recognized that I wouldn't get promoted for five more months. As an adult, the years seemed basically seamless, so again, I never saw much need to celebrate the end and the beginning of humankind's artificial measure of sequence. Consequently, my celebration of the New Year has always been limited to watching a few football games before retiring early so that I might take on whatever came next.

Yesterday was January 1. The commentators raved on about what a tough year we had just survived. Who could argue? Every sane human being would hope that the next twelve months would bring us less violence and more peace—topped off, of course, by a stronger market and bigger profits. After all, this is the American dream, and also the hope that drives the greeting that some of us offer each other every year: "Merry Christmas and a Prosperous New Year." From the culture's view, "happy" and "prosperous" are synonyms. The Bible speaks against this equation, but on this point the culture turns a deaf ear.

Your mom prepared rice and black-eyed peas yesterday. In the South, we have made black-eyed peas a symbol for good luck, with the result that many people would not think of entering the next twelve months without eating a batch on January 1. The rationale underlying this custom is that during the Civil War, the Federal troops destroyed the food crops of the Confederacy, but, for some reason, overlooked the ugly purple hulls of the hearty little black-eyed pea. Hence, the survivors of that terrible conflagration equated black-eyed peas with survival and good luck. Who could blame them?

Part of what I've learned on this journey out of myself and into the Spirit is to minimize the celebration of artificial measures of time and focus more on living in the moment. In teaching us to pray for our daily bread, Jesus was instructing us to do just that. As a friend is fond of saying, "The present is the present." This moment is the gift because God is in the present moment, active and always sovereign. And whether the calendar proclaims today to be January 1 or July 1, God is always the same—active and sovereign.

Every time I remember this truth, I sigh, relax, and say "thank you!" When I forget, I pick right up where I left off with the old habit of worry. These days, I find myself worrying far less as I celebrate the gift of this moment more than I ponder the possibilities—for good or for ill—of what lies ahead.

Coming Home

Dear Sarah,

WHAT DOES IT MEAN TO COME HOME? THAT IS AN IMPORTANT question. In fact, our general well-being may have everything to do with how we answer.

Years ago I was flying home from a day of lecturing at a theological seminary. I was tired and ready to sleep in my own bed. A flight attendant approached me and inquired as to my willingness to "look after" a five-year-old girl named Emily who for some reason flew with this carrier on a regular basis. I agreed, and within seconds Emily was presented to me.

Initially, this child defended herself with feigned indifference. My impression was that her young boundaries were both impenetrable and the consequence of heartache. I attempted a conversation, but Emily would have no part of it. She immediately turned away from me to stare through the porthole into darkness. I decided not to push and returned my attention to a book.

At takeoff, though, I felt her small hand touch mine. Still refusing to look at me, she announced, "I get scared at takeoffs, Mister. Can I hold your hand?"

I replied, "Emily, takeoffs sometimes scare me, too. Let's hold on to each other, and I believe we'll both feel better."

Once the plane reached cruising speed, Emily let go and turned away, again to stare at the night. Sometime after my first bag of peanuts, Emily surprised me with her second question of the night. "Mister," I heard her whisper, "do you know why God put the stars in the sky?"

"No, I guess I've never really considered that question before, Emily. Tell me, why did God put stars in the sky?" Again without turning to face me, she said, "Because they show us the way home."

As I considered the idea, I thought of Epiphany and three kings finding their way by following a star. Is this what it means to come home? I wondered to myself. I believe it must be. When I was a kid, I thought home was where my family lived. Once you were old enough to memorize and recite rote data, Sarah, your mom taught you your address in the event that you became separated from us. For you then, these numbers and words were home.

In college I read Robert Frost's definition of home as the place "where when you go there they have to take you in." After a decade of working with Dallas's homeless, I came to disagree with this cozy definition, for I know many men and even a few women who went somewhere only to find that they were no longer taken in.

So what is home? I think this is the most important question we can ask. Luke's Gospel defines home well in its tale of the prodigal who finally comes to himself, lifts himself out of the muck of a pigsty, and trudges home hungry, defeated, and so ashamed that he can scarcely think of anything to say other than "I have sinned." This story describes every human being's journey toward home. Luke writes: "So he set off and went to his father. But while he was still far off, his father saw him and was filled with compassion; he ran and put his arms around him and kissed him" (15:20).

God is home. The truth is that simple. All of us come from the same Parent—God, who is love. But because of our nature and in the wake of the complexities of our development as human beings, we necessarily lose sight of this truth as we first learn to defend and later to promote ourselves. Once we finally come to understand that we must be liberated from all bondage to the self, we begin the long journey home. This is the mystery, reflected in a star shining brightly in the winter sky, and this is the truth each of us must embrace if we ever hope to find our way home. If we claim to be "on the path," it would be wise for us to know where it is the path might take us. If it does not lead us home, it's the wrong path.

—Dad

The Right Attitude

Dear Sarah,

WHEN I WAS A KID, I WAS INFORMED MORE THAN ONCE THAT I HAD the wrong attitude. I never did learn what the right attitude might be, but I did, indeed, often hear that mine was flawed. My father was in sales for the whole of his career. When you sell anything for a living, a positive outlook on life would, I suspect, soon become essential. But one concomitant of capitalism is that optimism in this culture has been elevated to the rank of a religion and has even permeated some expressions of Christianity to the point that the gospel is equated with positive thinking.

I'm not opposed to positive thinking per se, but I'm leery of any belief system that denies reality. For example, optimism proved impotent in uncovering the Watergate scandal, in ending the Vietnam War, and in protecting this nation from the kind of wanton acts of terrorism we witnessed on September 11, 2001. So today I find myself cautious as opposed to automatically optimistic. I've come by this defense naturally through being lied to, and today I often tell people that I know very little, but I suspect a lot. In this culture, such is not the right attitude.

I find comfort in a question from the inspired genius of the apostle Paul (Galatians 1:10): "Am I now seeking human approval, or God's approval? Or am I trying to please people? If I were still pleasing people, I would not be a servant of Christ." To serve Christ means, among other things, to remain devoted to the truth at all costs. And, of course, if we are to speak and, even more important, live the truth, we may well offend a culture devoted to its interpretation of truth. But I'd much rather seek the truth than have others think well of me, be pleased with me, laud me, or include me in their fellowship.

When people tell me that they are either angry with me or, more euphemistically, inform me that they are disappointed in my attitude, I remind them that what they think of me is none of my business. I say this not to be flippant; rather, I offer this response because, through the teachings of Paul and the life of Jesus as portrayed in the four Gospels, I have come to the following two conclusions: (1) God's love for us never ends, and (2) the truth, no matter how tough it may be for us to swallow, is invariably worth speaking and, even more, a blessing to live.

Tossing the Shoe

Dear Sarah,

HIGH ABOVE THE STAGE OF DALLAS'S SUNSET HIGH SCHOOL SITS A forty-year-old tennis shoe that I "helped" toss to its final resting place so many years ago that I'd almost forgotten the incident. The ledge upon which this faded shoe is perched is no wider than six inches and serves as the frame for the immense stage thirty feet below. In the spring of 1964, when I was no more than a player in a collective game of cruelty, I joined other equally insecure boys in playing a game of "keep away" from a very wounded young man whom we deemed to be less than us and, therefore, unworthy of our friendship simply because he was overweight and clumsy. Our formula for success was simple and buttressed by the ocean of evidence gratuitously supplied by the culture.

Be judged cool, and you were "in" with us. Be dumb or awkward or pimply or poor or a person of color, and you were definitely "out." Be fat, and you were the sure target of our random abuse because, deep down, each one of us had been conditioned to believe that the single path to victory and personal acclaim lay in someone else's humiliation. This was our perspective, although, if pressed, each of us would have claimed to be a Christian.

Unfortunately, the pudgy sophomore we called "Piglet" stumbled into our lair one morning in the school auditorium when no teachers were available to protect him from our spontaneous demonstration of barbarity. Within seconds we were upon him from every side like so many lions tearing at an antelope. We ripped away a cloth bag containing his gym clothes and discovered two tennis shoes. Someone began tossing one of the shoes around the room, and immediately our attack turned to a deeper mortification. We grunted like hyenas as we tossed the shoe to one another and this frustrated boy tried to retrieve his property. We all knew that if he showed up in gym class without his shoes, he would suffer the dreaded whack of the coach's paddle. And if he cried, the coach would hit him mercilessly until he either passed out or quit crying.

One of my buddies tossed the shoe as high as he could, and the thing appeared to disprove Newton's Law of Gravitation because what went up this time failed to come down. Stunned, all of us, including our victim, gazed skyward to discover that the shoe was now balanced on the six-inch ledge of the stage's frame. The "tosser" was impressed with his prowess and declared, "[Expletive deleted] I couldn't do that again if I tried."

The bell rang and we dashed away to our respective classrooms, leaving our victim to dread his certain date with the paddle. We gave him not a second thought, because in our perception, his loss was not our problem. After all, the punishment would befall him, not us.

Four decades after this incident, I happened into the auditorium of my alma mater and was startled to see the shoe still there, where our unkindness had landed it. Try as I might, I could not recall the name of the student we once tortured in that very room. After getting past the amazement that the shoe had remained perched on the ledge after all these years, I was so overcome with shame that I sat down in one of the old wooden chairs that has held students for more than seventy-five years, bowed my head, and tried asking God for forgiveness. But no prayer would flow. Shame blocked my intention as if it were a boulder holding back a torrent. I trembled as I tried to imagine the pain we had inflicted upon an innocent young man. I then recalled Mark Twain's proclamation that one "cannot pray a lie." Being youthful and immature was no excuse for the pain I had caused a fellow student, nor was being a sinner. In this very room, I had willingly hurt another human being in the pathological attempt to build myself up by seeing someone else suffer. This is the worst we can do to one another, and I did it.

As I rose, I decided that grace has to be something very radical and real; otherwise, how could anyone ever grow past guilt. In the holy presence of grace, I made the only prayer I could. I prayed that the boy I hurt so many years ago might forgive me. Although I knew I didn't deserve his forgiveness, I dared, nevertheless, to ask for it, and grace arrived like a warm quilt to cover me until my trembling ceased.

The Whereabouts of God

Dear Sarah,

RUBEN MUST BE MIDDLE-AGED BY NOW, BUT WHEN I KNEW HIM HE was a mentally challenged black kid who lived with his aunt in the housing projects in Missouri.

I came to view Ruben as a sage. Although he was judged by his teachers to be slow, I discovered him to be wise. Once he and I both saw a brawl at an American Legion baseball game during which both benches emptied. From our safe vantage point in the bleachers, I turned to Ruben and casually asked, "Well, what do you think of that?" He offered his trademark grin, which featured more teeth than appeared possible to be crowded into one small mouth, and said, "If you can't get along, then get along."

One summer afternoon, Ruben and I strolled past the reconstructed seventeenth-century Christopher Wren chapel on the campus of the town's Presbyterian college. The Germans had all but destroyed this London church in the Second World War, but what remained of its shell was brought to this American campus and rebuilt brick by brick. Long before I came to his town, Ruben had watched this little chapel being restored not a block from his home in the housing projects.

Ruben paused to ponder this perfectly rebuilt empty edifice casting a pleasant shadow on the both of us and asked, "Does God live in there?" I responded, "No, I think God lives inside of you and inside of me and also outside of us and always with us."

"Like up in the sky?" Ruben asked.

"Yeah, Ruben, like up in the sky."

"Like down in my belly?" he questioned, as he yanked up his snow cone–stained T-shirt and rubbed his round tummy.

"There, too, I suspect."

"You mean at home with us?" he asked. I nodded.

"God Almighty!" he squealed. "Just wait 'til I get home and tell my auntie that God stays with us and the rats over in the projects when he could live right here in this fine little church."

Every time I hear the word *Immanuel,* which means "God with us," I think of my friend Ruben, and I recall his wisdom.

—Dad

Dwindle Down

Dear Sarah,

I RECEIVED E-MAIL YESTERDAY MORNING FROM A FRIEND WHO ASKED permission to nominate me for a community award. My ego became immediately excited. "Wow!" I whispered. "Everyone in this town is finally going to see what an altruistic man I am. I'll be praised and applauded and, perhaps, even become known for my generosity." I could hardly wait to shoot an E-mail back to my friend telling her to proceed with the nomination with haste and employ the sum of her persuasive powers. After all, in my own always-skewed estimation I have, indeed, done a great deal for the nonprofit organization she serves.

My ego was ready to make the dash toward illusory fame. Then I recalled the word *dwindle,* which is attached to the following elegance from Thomas Merton (*New Seeds of Contemplation* [New York, 1961], p. 182):

> The joy of the mystical love of God springs from a liberation from all self-hood by the annihilation of every trace of pride. Desire not to be exalted but only to be abased, not to be great but only little in your own eyes and in the eyes of the world; for the only way to enter into that joy is to dwindle down to a vanishing point and become absorbed in God through the center of your own nothingness. The only way to possess His greatness is to pass through the needle's eye of your own absolute insufficiency.

A wise friend's definition of fame as "the adoration of strangers" came to mind. Did I want that? No. What, then, did I want? The Spirit answered, "To serve God."

I told my friend, "Thank you, but no thank you." Deep down, though, I hoped she would insist, and then I could cave in to her pressure and feign reticence. Thankfully, she wrote back immediately and said, "Okay, we will remove your name from our list."

To say that I'm glad I came to this decision would be to lie. I was thankful that I sometimes remember the truth that what little good I do is never about me. At least now I know that, thank God.

—Dad

Talking to a Dog About God

Dear Sarah,

MY NEIGHBOR IS A SAVIOR. HE IS NOT MY SAVIOR, BUT HE IS definitely the salvation of Baby Dog. He discovered this black Chow Chow puppy in the Hill Country scrub close to where we live across the blacktop road from each other. Unspeakable cruelty had fastened her small body to a cedar post, where the marks on her bushy hide made it obvious that she had been scorched repeatedly with a welder's torch. It is a wonder she survived, and the truth is that she would not have lived had my neighbor not happened upon her. But by grace and good fortune, or both, he did. And because of his willingness to take her into his unceasing care, she not only survived, but also thrived, although with permanent scars in her black fur and on her tender psyche.

Baby Dog is fiercely loyal to my neighbor. She will greet me with a half nod now and then, but I can pet her only when he is around. In the days before he retired, when travel marked this man's lifestyle, I often fed Baby Dog. But she would never eat until I had filled one bowl with dried food, poured fresh water into another, and then moved on. As I walked away, I could hear her munching with what I suspected was one eye trained on me.

Over the years, Baby Dog has come to trust me enough to stand in the road as I haul a week's worth of garbage past her lookout. She dare not risk a relationship by looking at me; nevertheless, she permits me to pass without offering so much as a counterfeit snarl.

One night, years ago, I stood in the path where I regularly haul garbage and focused my naked gaze upon that tentative phenomenon we knew that year as Comet Hale-Bopp. As this starry wonder stretched before me, a magnificence that could only be measured in light years, I dropped my eyes momentarily and spied Baby Dog waddling toward me, no doubt driven by equal parts curiosity and boredom. "Hello," I offered to her typically silent rebuff. Studying again the spectacle high above, I inquired, "Baby Dog, just how much do you know about comets?"

"About as much as you do about the One who makes them."

—Dad

No Longer Believing in God

Dear Sarah,

I NO LONGER BELIEVE IN GOD, FOR BELIEVING IN GOD, OR IN ANY-thing else, involves a cognitive process that is limited to the realm of ideas. I believe in light switches turning on, if, that is, the electric bill has been paid, and I believe in my pickup running as long as I keep the old thing tuned up and the oil changed. Further, I believe that in a very few weeks, regardless of whether or not that old groundhog up in Pennsylvania sees his shadow, winter will slip into spring and the bluebonnets will bloom in the Hill Country. I believe that Easter will follow, the baseball season will crank up, and one more humid Texas summer will impose its unrelenting heat upon us for longer than any season should hang around. Those are some of the things I believe in, but I no longer believe in God.

When I was a seminary student, I certainly believed in God. Had I not believed in God, I would have been kicked out of the school and dismissed as a candidate for ordination. Consequently, every chance I got, I was quick to say to those in authority, "You bet I believe in God." And the fact is that I so believed in God that I learned to speak of God with so much eloquence that I impressed myself with my mastery of the "God constructs." With the best of them, I referred frequently to such high-sounding ideas as the "ground of all being," the "transcendent other," and the notion of "pure God consciousness."

Decades would pass before I would come to understand that believing in God is about as useless as not believing in God. An ancient psalmist calls us to "be still and know that I am God." As strange as it sounds, this admonition has very little, if anything, to do with thinking. Notice here what the psalmist does not say—"Be still and believe that I am God"— because knowing is a process that is much deeper and far richer than merely believing in something.

Knowing involves our full being, including our soul, and our journey into knowing affects every level of us so profoundly that we cannot possibly describe it. The best we can do once we experience this mystery of knowing is to declare that we experience truth in the very core of our being.

For someone who has not experienced what it means to know, this makes little sense. Those who know the truth have had their eyes opened, and for the first time in their life, they know what they see because they have, through hard work and discipline, come to discover a good bit about what they truly are. The result of this work is that they know that they are loved and that they are evolving slowly but surely toward making their lives an authentic expression of love.

I recognize that there are other places in Scripture in which we are commanded to believe. In John 3:16, we are reminded that everyone who believes in Jesus as the Son of God will not perish. Nevertheless, from my perspective, believing is still less than knowing. Believing generates the silky eloquence of the Pharisees, which is nothing more than an expression of the honed ego. Real knowing, though, is the mystical process that opens our eyes for the first time to the truth of who we really are and simultaneously to the radical grace of God. This is why Jesus once said to the Pharisees, "But now that you say, 'We see,' your sin remains." And perhaps this is also why tears come to my eyes every time I sing the lines, "I was blind, but now I see."

—Dad

Subtle Sounds

Dear Sarah,

I ENJOY THE SUBTLE SOUNDS: RAIN DROPPING THROUGH BARE January branches, a sigh, the flutter of a white-winged dove's wing, a breeze traveling where it will, or a doe signaling with tail raised high as she dashes through the brush toward the illusion of safety.

Elijah learned to listen beyond the subtle sounds. Perhaps this is why he bore the name he did, for his name means literally "lover of Yahweh." It is obvious that he loved enough to discipline himself to listen and finally to hear the truth.

Elijah was told by God to "go out and stand on the mountain before the LORD, for the LORD is about to pass by.' Now there was a great wind, so strong that it was splitting mountains and breaking rocks in pieces before the LORD, but the LORD was not in the wind; and after the wind an earthquake . . . and after the earthquake a fire, but the LORD was not in the fire; and after the fire a sound of sheer silence. When Elijah heard it, he wrapped his face in his mantle and went out and stood at the entrance of the cave" (1 Kings 19:11-13). And here, the King James Version translates what Elijah heard to read "a still small voice" instead of "a sheer silence."

A rabbi friend tells me that a better translation of the Hebrew is this: "The silence was so profound it actually spoke." I find this perspective both intriguing and inviting. Since I first heard it, I have sometimes wondered if I would not enhance my spiritual growth if I, like Elijah, disciplined myself to listen to the silence. But I'm not Elijah, and I find it difficult to hear the silence, though I do often listen to it. And it is in this daily discipline that I hear and so enjoy the subtle sounds of life.

A friend I long ago joined in opening a soup kitchen in Dallas claims that the only way to hear anything worth hearing is not with the ears, but with the heart. I suspect this man is right because the way we have structured this culture is apparently to embrace as truth the unexamined conviction that noise—preaching, singing, teaching, praying out loud, and debating one another about God or the way the church should go—is what it means to be religious. Elijah's dramatic experience, however, instructs us that the truth is not to be found in the big noises.

To love, we must first hear. And to hear, we must listen—to our own interior lives, to the words of others, to the subtle sounds of this world, and, most of all, to the silence. It is in the silence that truth shows up and sometimes even whispers.

—Dad

Glimpsing God

Dear Sarah,

MORE THAN THIRTY YEARS AGO I WAS SENT TO VISIT A DALLAS psychologist in the cause of being examined for ordination. For two days, this woman's assistant administered a battery of tests that required a great deal of effort on my part. I was close to exhausted when I finished.

When I finally met with the psychologist, she glared at me and said, among other things, "Mr. Lively, you're not nearly as smart as you think you are."

I sat before this woman feeling suddenly ashamed and, if you will, "found out." Stammering, I responded, "Ma'am, I don't think of myself as smart at all. In fact, I've known bird dogs smarter than I happen to be on my best days." She didn't appear amused. Next she posed this question: "Why do you want to go into the ministry?"

This time I considered my response carefully because I sensed that a great deal rode on the answer. Finally I muttered what I knew I was supposed to say: "Because I believe God has called me into this work." Her affect remained as frozen as new ice.

In those days I possessed no real confidence and, consequently, I parroted what I thought those in authority wanted to hear. Today my answer would be, "Doctor, I saw something in my twentieth summer of life that spoke to me of an amazing truth without words."

At this point I fantasize the following curt response, "And what, may I ask, did you see?"

I climbed out of a one-man tent that I had pitched the night before on Danner Hill in the Colorado Rockies, ten thousand feet above sea level. The morning was brisk and the buffalo grass cold and still damp with dew as I traipsed toward a plump mare, grazing knee deep in high-country succulence. I climbed on her broad, bare back and struck her flank once with my heel as I guided her with my knees up the mountain. We rode through a thick fir forest, with every branch swatting at me as though punishment was to be the painful cost of our slow ascent. In time, we happened upon a pristine cataract pouring its life passionately forth to feed the world below with the sweetness of snowmelt.

I raised my empty tin cup high as I slipped from the mare's smooth back. Stepping toward the water's deafening roar, I dropped to my knees in the sandy mud and dipped my cup into the water. Withdrawing it, I placed it to my lips and drank of something so pure and so refreshing as to make me glad in that moment that I was alive, young, healthy, and filled to the brim with questions. I dipped the cup a second time and this time poured its cold contents over my bare head.

And that's when it happened. Without any awareness, I baptized myself. I'd been baptized in a Presbyterian church sanctuary when I was three months old, but I knew nothing of the experience or of the One in whose name I had been promised. But on this morning, I poured cold-mountain water over my thinning hair and I sensed something I'd never before felt. Even today I can't describe it beyond the perhaps overused idea of truth. Suffice it to say, the stream became to me a symbol of all that was good and right, and I was its humble supplicant, washing from my head the sins of selfishness and participating for one brief moment in the currents of eternity.

Above where I balanced upon muddy knees, a bull elk stepped from the shadowed woods and bowed as though joining me in supplication before also partaking of the snow's melted bounty. "Good morning," I whispered. But the creature failed to see me, much less hear my greeting above the river's roar.

"May I remain here for a moment," I asked. The big bull

appeared to vote in the affirmative as he lifted his rack toward the sky's first light. His nod was all the encouragement I required to realize that for the rest of my life I wanted to be about the work of something wondrous and beautiful whose purpose it was to bring life to those below.

So, as strange as it seems, I believe that an elk and a waterfall called me into the ministry.

Had I shared this story with that already surly psychologist, she would no doubt have rejected my petition for candidacy. But today I offer it to you, Sarah, because I know you will hear it and understand.

The Ordination

Dear Sarah,

I WAS ORDAINED IN BATESVILLE, ARKANSAS, EXACTLY FIVE MONTHS to the day before your arrival in this old world. At the time of my ordination, an enormous rift in the church was beginning to show itself. It's always been there, but because of the imminent reunification of the church after more than a century of separation following the Civil War, this latest contention was fueled by fear on the part of self-proclaimed "evangelicals." Many had convinced themselves that a small army of so-called liberals (like me) had entered seminary to avoid the draft, not to mention their patriotic duty in Vietnam. Worse yet, in their view, these left-wing pariahs would soon graduate, pass the stringent ordination exams, receive calls from unsuspecting churches, and forever pollute the pristine Presbyterian Church.

I had no idea that I was walking into the most painful challenge I'd yet faced when I entered a candidate's committee meeting. A Dallas layman, whom I would later discover so opposed change that even a hint of some new idea turned him reactively punitive, chaired this body. This man's eyes were permanently squinted, drawing his wrinkled face into a scowl, and his lips were thin and so pursed that I suspected that even the slightest expressions of kindness might find it impossible to escape his seemingly permanent sour disposition.

He averted his eyes as I strode confidently into the room, causing me to worry some, but not much. I was far too naive about politics to realize that this man was on the threshold of playing the time-honored game of "Gotcha." And in the parlance of my childhood, and unbeknownst to me, I was "it."

Only later would I learn that I had been singled out because I was student body president and had written a few unpublished, but still circulated, pieces bearing definite liberal leanings.

I decided not to be buffaloed by this Christian, and I stared at him while he kept his gaze averted and his agenda hidden. Though I was only twenty-six, I decided to take this man on. Whatever this fellow's game, I was up to it. He was at least twice my age and had reportedly already made a fortune peddling something in Dallas.

As I pondered him, I wondered: What caused him to be so frightened? What had turned him so dour and apparently so bitter? Who had appointed this frightened fellow the gatekeeper to Christ's church? And was not the church the future tense of love residing squarely, though always enigmatically, in the present?

Once the meeting was called to order, his agenda surfaced. He more attacked than quizzed me. After he was done with a barrage of humiliating remarks aimed straight at my character and faith, I placed my head on the table as questions raced through my mind regarding whether or not I should go through with this pursuit. I'd invested four years of study and had successfully completed all of the requirements for both graduation and ordination, and yet, in that gloomy moment, I could not see myself moving forward. I prayed, but no answer returned to comfort me. I came precariously close to standing and declaring, "Look, Mister! I've given four years of my life to the enterprise of theological education. I will graduate with honors in a few weeks, and I've already passed all of the ordination exams. If you are an example of what the church is, I want no part of it. I want nothing to do with your fear, and neither do I want any part of your repressed rage. Nor will I accept the unconscious garbage you have heaped upon my head for the past hour. No, sir, if you're the church, you can have it!"

Fortunately, I did not throw those words at him, but I sure

did think them. Sadly enough, I've thought them many times in the past thirty years because I've experienced enough fear and projection and pettiness in the church to make me hear the veracity in Karl Barth's famous declaration that the Bible's message is that "God must hate religion." Even so, these painful episodes have taught me to turn the other cheek and to pray especially for those who loathe themselves enough to trick themselves into believing they despise me or anyone else.

How tragic this condition is in us. But until we become conscious, I suspect we will continue to operate out of the ego and make the terrible mistake of viewing our personal agendas as God's holy will.

—*Dad*

The Church

Dear Sarah,

TRUTH CANNOT BE ORGANIZED AND NEITHER, I SUSPECT, CAN LOVE. Nevertheless, twenty centuries ago, people founded the church, attributed to God the form this establishment eventually assumed, and thereafter began making up rules and peddling the notion that love can somehow be mediated through an institution.

It cannot. Only individuals can express love and discover the truth. No institution can do that simply because, by nature, institutions require consensus. Consensus is invariably the product of a political process, and politics is the province of the ego. No one expresses love or actually experiences truth's depth from the ego, for these gifts come to us only from the Spirit. The moment we attempt to organize them, codify them, or sell them, they are lost.

Nevertheless, we have the church and, too often it seems, it has us. I cannot tell you how many men and women have told me over the past three decades that the church has hurt them. What they mean most often is that individuals within the institution have exploited or wounded them. On a few occasions, I've even heard of people being abused by collections of individuals, or councils, who were wedded to groupthink and who appeared to find some kind of satisfaction in ganging up on others.

Last Saturday, I received a form letter from the denominational office inviting me to attend a meeting in San Antonio next month. At this special called meeting, two commissions will be elected to "look into" the difficulties of two churches.

My eyes ached when they happened upon these sad words.

Although I have no idea regarding the specifics of these difficulties, I do know the cause. Regardless of the systemic dynamics extant in any situation, the genesis of our difficulties is always the same—the ego.

The ego has an insatiable need to be right. This is the self-affirming cycle by which it exists and thrives. Both in the church and in the world at large, our egos are inflated every time someone or a group points in our direction and says, "You are so right!" With sufficient inflation, we can even come to believe that we are meant to control everything, including God's church.

Spiritual people, however, have given up the need to be right. They have dedicated their energy, instead, to doing what is right. For them, doing what is right is always synonymous with love.

I won't attend the meeting in San Antonio, but I will definitely pray for the people in those churches that are currently experiencing difficulty. My prayer will be as succinct as it will be simple, and it will be the same prayer I offer each new morning: "God, please release me (and us) from bondage to self. Amen."

—*Dad*

Being Called

Dear Sarah,

WHEN I WAS A KID, I CLOSELY WATCHED THE VARIOUS DEMONSTRATIONS of adoration young men in our church would be shown once they made the difficult decision to enter the ministry. To a man (no women, it seems, were "called" by God in those days), they claimed that the Almighty had been hammering at them for years, even harder than a used car salesman, in the noble cause of convincing them that they must be pressed into holy service. So always reluctantly, and at great personal sacrifice (about which they were eagerly loquacious), they accepted our collective good wishes before they trudged off to the seminary in Austin.

When my time came, I simply stood up and said, "God has called me." For two hours thereafter on a cold February Sunday afternoon, men (and, again, no women) pummeled me with questions. Finally, the church elders decided that I might be declared a candidate for the ministry.

If there was any fanfare or applause, I failed to recognize it.

One old man, a veteran of the First World War and long a faithful churchman, asked, "Are you just hiding from the draft in aiming to attend seminary?" Deep down I knew I should respond to this man's chilling question with a resounding "Yes." Of course I was doing what I could to escape the madness of Southeast Asia. I also knew, however, that if I told the truth in February of 1969, I'd be denied the opportunity to hide in the seminary until either this war blew over or I was "forced" into ordination, whichever came first.

I lied. I claimed to be called when the only real call I knew anything about on that day was the one to save my life so that I might in some small way come to discover the truth.

But as it turns out, I don't think I lied at all. I just suspected I did because I was too young, too immature, too starved for recognition and praise, and far too narcissistic even to begin to understand that every authentic call is a voice outside of us that summons each of us to venture beyond ourselves and toward the discovery of ultimate truth. So, in that sense I was "called" because every human being is called.

Of course, not everyone takes off for seminary, thank God, but in the sense that every human being is made for love, every one of us is called. And for the past thirty years I've remained more or less on the road that leads out of the preoccupation with myself and toward what it means to become the living expression of love. I've meandered all over the map, but by grace, I've always found my way back to the path.

During your first summer of life, Sarah, I ventured off to a tiny burg in Arkansas scarcely large enough to support a Presbyterian church. As was my habit, I located the church two hours before the scheduled service and then began an even more earnest search for the first greasy spoon I could find open on an early Sunday morning.

I happened into a diner in which the requisite table of gawking farmers studied me like I possessed the potential of a prize bull. A man behind the counter spotted my black Bible stuffed with a sermon manuscript and asked in a loud voice, "You some kind of a preacher?"

My affirmative nod earned me a second question: "Well, are you one of them called preachers, or are you one of them educated preachers?"

I smiled uncomfortably as the smoky room awaited my answer. Once again I felt as though some ordination committee was grilling me. I walked slowly to a counter stool, sat down, and said, "Well, right now, I reckon I'm far more educated than called. But I've learned to pray for the call, gentlemen. And I pray for it every day." My response seemed to disarm them to the point that the room was once more filled with rumblings about the government and the sky's adamant refusal to bless their crops with even so much as a drop of rain.

—Dad

Sadness

Dear Sarah,

I DON'T UNDERSTAND THE SADNESS THREATENING TO OVERWHELM me, though the doctors tell me it may have to do with the medication I'm required to take. The fact is, I find it terribly uncomfortable. When this sadness arrives, which is often since I was diagnosed with heart disease, I find myself longing to curl up and rest in the simple hope that life will go on, at least for a while, and that I might continue to make small contributions to the kingdom. So far, the signs appear favorable. Nevertheless, the sadness visits most afternoons when low blood sugar, or whatever it is, seems to make me vulnerable to my old, always unhealthful, habit of worrying.

Yesterday afternoon, I got up from the office chair and felt better immediately. Encouraged, I walked toward the parking lot without explanation or even a hint of guilt. Once inside the car, I turned on the music and listened to Townes Van Zandt singing one of his love poems before I put the car in gear. I was several miles down the highway before I chose to venture west and deep into Hill Country.

Forty-five miles later, I found myself caught in the slight bustle that is quaint Blanco. There I paused before the marquee of what decades before had been this town's only picture show. Tears welled again in my eyes as I read congratulations to the Blanco Panthers for winning the state class 2-A title in football. Sometimes the oddest things make me cry.

I thanked God that boys still play football, that cheerleaders cheer them on, and that somewhere amidst a long roll of hills interrupted only by the timeless persistence of rivers, people plow the rocky earth, raise livestock, and live close to the land in harmony with the seasons. On Sundays they bow down before God; on the other six days they rear sons who know how to play hard on Friday night.

A half step out of my latest bout of self-pity, I recalled my youth, grinned at the sun setting into the cold waters of the Blanco River, and thanked God for it all—even my sadness. It is in this desperate, lonely place inside of me that, strangely, I sometimes discover what Jesus called "the kingdom of heaven." Perhaps living through this sadness is the only way to find it.

—Dad

Fear

Dear Sarah,

YEARS AGO, I LEANED UPON THE CHAIN-LINK FENCE THAT DEFINES the borders of the cemetery in which scores of our ancestors are buried in the sandy loam of East Texas. I was young and scarcely self-aware; nevertheless, I dared to make the decision that from that day forward I would give up being afraid.

Naïveté was my shield, and my sword was the ridiculous and culturally sanctioned conviction that, with sufficient insight, I possessed the power to exorcise my personal demons. After all, this was the pretentious age of self-help, during which every wounded ego was being encouraged on most fronts, including the church, to become "actualized" with little if any regard to the consequences. Sensitivity training was the rage, and encounter groups became the arena by which all hip dialogue occurred.

My decision proved impotent even before I departed that sacred red dirt, for I'd no more than switched on the ignition of my Volkswagen when worry once more returned to intimidate me. I screamed only to hear fear's taunt. "You'll never be free of me!" the old devil roared.

Decades later, I learned in the first Alcoholics Anonymous meeting I attended that God can (and even longs to) restore us to sanity. This revelation spawned two new questions. The first was summed up in the word, *How?* And the second was, *What exactly is sanity?*

Once I came to think of God as the Mystery that is love, the urgency of the first question diminished. For the first time, a new serenity vied with my old companion, angst, for possession of my soul. Through that struggle, I slowly came to see that to be sane means to make of one's life an authentic expression of love. Sane people know so well what it means to love that, in time, compassion becomes their true identity. This is what John means when he tells us that "love casts out fear."

So today, in place of holding on to fear as an ineffectual habit, I think, instead, of loving the man who "broke" in line in front of me last night at the cafeteria, or I form kind thoughts regarding everyone waiting with me in the reception area at the hospital, or I pray daily for the woman who comes to my office each Friday whose thinking is so fragmented that I find it painful to spend an hour with her, or I offer forgiveness to a man who went out of his way to injure me ten years ago. The more I consciously express love, the more peace seems to find its way into my heart. And, as bizarre as it sounds, from somewhere beyond me I occasionally even hear a voice whisper, "This, my friend, is sanity."

—*Dad*

Light

Dear Sarah,

THE PROLOGUE OF JOHN'S GOSPEL INSPIRES US WITH THIS SMALL, but still amazing, proclamation: "The light shines in the darkness, and the darkness did not overcome it" (1:5). Then in chapter 11, John tells a tale that, to the immature, represents a hope vouchsafed by history and, to the cynical, a claim so far-fetched as to make one reject every other mention of miracles.

Both responses are wrong. Chapter 11 tells of Jesus' raising his friend Lazarus, who had been dead for four days and whose decomposing corpse had begun to stink. The man's sisters, Mary and Martha, had sent for Jesus when their beloved brother first showed symptoms portending a deadly illness. For some inexplicable reason, Jesus tarried, and his friend died. Once Jesus arrives at the deceased man's village, a wide place in the road called Bethany, he literally calls the dead man out of the tomb, a dark cave, and restores his life.

If we make literalism an issue, we miss the point. This event may have occurred precisely as John tells it, but for me, this possibility is not important. What really matters is the truth that love is light, and this light possesses the power to penetrate every form of darkness in the cause of restoring even the most wounded and self-loathing human being to the fullness of life. In this sense, John's story of the resurrection of Lazarus is the "fleshing out" of the Gospel's earlier proclamation that "the light shines in the darkness, and the darkness did not overcome it."

This is the best news I know, and in both counseling and preaching, I share it often. Fear breeds darkness, which all too easily can turn to evil, but love is always the giver of light, which is the only gift sufficiently powerful to liberate the human spirit from self-inflicted death. We may be walking around drawing breath, but if we do not live in the light that is the conscious decision to make of our lives an expression of love, we are either dying spiritually or already dead.

Love penetrates the darkness of the unconscious caves we inhabit and it always calls our soul out. This is love's purpose, and once we become conscious of the truth that we were made for the light, we live in a way that calls others out as well.

Years ago, I crawled under the pier and beam foundation of a derelict icehouse in South Dallas to do what I could for a pitiful young man who had decided to drink himself to death. I checked for a pulse and, finding one, began dragging him from the shadows. Within a half hour, he was admitted to Parkland Memorial Hospital, where days later he experienced what he would come to describe as an epiphany. As he lay in a bed in the indigent wing of the hospital, he claimed that a light had appeared to him and said, "Harry, you can live or you can die. The choice is yours."

Harry chose to live, and more than twenty years later, I joined a throng of friends in celebrating this man's ordination as a deacon in the Episcopal Church. As I accepted from his hand the chalice of wine, which he assured me was the blood of Christ, I trembled in his presence. If anyone were to tell me today that he or she didn't believe that Jesus really raised a man from the dead, I would say, "Oh, yes, he did! I was there and I witnessed the miracle of resurrection with my own eyes."

—Dad

Competition

Dear Sarah,

RECENTLY, AN ARTIST FRIEND DREW A PORTRAIT OF ME WITH NOTHING more than a pencil and paper. I was so taken aback by her rendering of me that I literally felt my heart pounding when I first saw it. She so captured my spirit that I spent the longest time studying the face staring back at me as I searched for insight in the rendering peering at me from the paper. The face was mine, but the features seemed far more interesting than I've ever thought myself to be. Likely, this experience was one more expression of narcissism; nevertheless, I found myself pondering for the longest time the depth in this man's eyes.

A day or so later, the artist called to respond to the several E-mails I'd shot at her thanking her profusely for her gift. That's when she told me that someone she knows is jealous of her work and strives feverishly to best her as an artist.

Why do we do this to one another and, even more puzzling, to ourselves? I'm not sure I possess the wisdom from which any satisfactory answer may be drawn, yet, I wrestle.

Some competition is good because, among other things, it holds prices down, pumps up the interest rates, and turns ordinary weekends into festivals for folks in the fall once college football gets under way. But like all things, competition definitely has its limits; and every time it is viewed as a means of self-definition, it becomes, at best, problematic and, at worst, spiritually virulent.

The wise among us have given up being competitive because they no longer feel the need to be defined as "best" or "great" or, worse yet, " a living legend." They are content to be and to enjoy expressing their gifts in the assurance that they are loved. These few know that love, like grace, is always sufficient, and they will be the first to tell you that "best" is a myth that spurs us on to certain misery. These people would much rather collaborate than compete. They find their joy in cooperating with others and giving God the glory, which is where it always belongs, anyway.

I once heard a Christian announce publicly that some institution had selected him as one of the best writers of contemporary spirituality in the entire world. I thought it sad that any institution would so misunderstand the real nature of spiritual expression as to view it as a contest. I saw it as tragic that any man who writes in the name of him who called all of us to meekness would draw attention to his own imperfect efforts. But the ego is always a powerful force, and its need for stroking is insatiable, I suspect. Perhaps this is why Jesus offered us the paradox that the discovery of one's true self happens only in the wake of forever losing who we have made ourselves to be.

—Dad

Being the Best

Dear Sarah,

THE LAST TEN-KILOMETER RACE I RAN WAS IN DALLAS IN FEBRUARY 1987. After that, my back ached often, and my knees sometimes felt as though needles were being pushed into the cartilage. I gave up running for the safer discipline of walking.

It was during that final race that I experienced a brush with revelation. A young girl who wore the track uniform of Sunset High School, my alma mater, ran behind me for the first mile or so, and her stride seemed as effortless as the swing of a clock's pendulum. Her feet hit the pavement in a rhythm that suggested a pace I knew I could not possibly keep up for very long. But right there I decided that I couldn't let this schoolgirl best me. After all, she was no more than sixteen.

My pride was pitted against her training, and there was no contest. Compared to her, I was old and far less fit. Consequently, I watched her draw even with me with an easy gait that portended an early finish. As I saw her gaining on me, this command arrived: "Do your best!"

I pushed harder, and once more the young girl drew even with me. A second time I pushed and looked up in time to see her running past me. Shame mixed with thoughts of defeat, and the admonition to do my best was lost in the sound of her quick steps.

For the remainder of those six miles, I wondered whether I had actually done my best. The possibilities proved sobering, for had I driven myself to best a kid at least twenty years my junior, who likely made running a lifestyle. I could easily have ruptured my spleen, blown my heart, or done permanent damage to an already-aching back.

Days later, I recognized that I had driven myself to "do my best" because I'd been conditioned by the culture to do just that—my very best. Further, I decided that the goal of "best" could contain a dangerous message, though I do believe that it is noble for all of us to stretch in the cause of excellence. But stretching toward excellence and "doing our best" strike me as different.

I've had the admonition "just do your best" hurled at me all of my life, and, most often, it is attached to some expression of encouragement that sounds like this: "It doesn't really matter if you win that game or pass that examination, just do your best."

On the surface, these words sound like good advice. But one problem with this, in the main, unexamined idea is that there is no "best." The ideal of being "best" is for the most part a myth that is much like a desert mirage: the closer we get to it, the more distant it appears. Sadly, the goal of best has driven many a man, woman, and child to the point of despair, shame, heartache, and, worse yet, suicide, because it is precariously close to the notion that we are justified in the eyes of God and those who profess to love us if only we do our best.

Fifteen years after this race, I was given a free weekend in the Texas Hill Country that coincided with my newspaper column deadline. Because I did not own a laptop at the time, I packed a writing pad and a couple of pens and promised myself that I would produce the column after I fished, canoed, hiked, napped, and performed every other activity I could manufacture. As the weekend rapidly drew to a close, the pad of paper remained as blank as my imagination. I possessed not so much as one idea about what I would write, and as the wee hours of Monday morning arrived to taunt me, I wrote these three words at the top of the page: "Do your best!" Immediately thereafter I jotted one of the weakest columns I've ever written, and, of course, the topic was the myth of the standard we so casually refer to as "best." I concluded the piece with this disclaimer. "This is not my best work."

The column appeared in the *Austin American-Statesman* sometime before Christmas that year, and the piece was what

I regarded as something between eminently forgettable and downright awful. Two months passed, and on a sleet-filled February morning, I received a phone call at my office from a husky voice asking, "Are you the man who wrote that piece in the paper who claims that we don't have to do our best?"

My initial thought was to deny everything. I couldn't decide if I was embarrassed to admit to writing that column or if I felt I had somehow betrayed a cultural value as sacred as patriotism, motherhood, and baseball. I stalled for time until the voice asked a second, and far more poignant, question. "May I come see you?"

Days later, a woman who bore the obvious signs of depression appeared in my office. Her eyes reflected sadness the way rain puddles hold light at night. The lines in her face told a story of despair without any need for words. And from her posture, even as she sat, she appeared to have been bearing a heavy sack of rocks on her shoulders for years. I asked, "What can I do for you?"

Her response stunned me: "I'm a psychiatrist. And I was sitting alone in my office dangerously close to committing suicide when I read your idea that 'best' is a ridiculous myth. For some reason, I thought you might, at the very least, be willing to hear the depth of my pain."

I assured her that I was, indeed, willing, and within the hour, and with her permission, I was able to connect her to a psychiatrist who immediately hospitalized her.

If there is a point to this story, I suppose it is that God can make use of our honesty, but likely can do very little with the hubris within us that peddles as truth nonsense like that insidious little message of doing our best.

Paul wrote, "[God's] power is made perfect in weakness." As far as I am concerned, that insight forever silences every cultural voice that screams at us the error that we haven't anything at all unless we have done our best.

—*Dad*

Integrity

Dear Sarah,

THE EMANCIPATION PROCLAMATION WAS ISSUED EIGHTY-THREE years before my birth, but its liberating words had not yet fully penetrated the myths or illumined the dark shadow of racism in East Texas by the time I entered this world. In fact, I remember hearing adults use the "n" word as unselfconsciously as if they were referring to a breed of cow or a hog. The "n" word was a well-worn, and always derisive, sobriquet in the culture that reared me and seared my soul with its myriad lies. The greatest lie attached to that always injurious word was the myth of racial inferiority.

Grapeland, Texas, was not big enough or sufficiently prosperous to qualify as a county seat; yet it, like most towns in the post–Reconstruction South, laid claim to an institution that was designed from the get-go to perpetuate the theory of black inferiority—the quarter. The ignoble and little-questioned proposition of black inferiority contained two basic tenets: (1) slavery may have been a bit harsh at times, but American Negroes were better off having come to this continent, even if by slave ship, than they would have been had they remained in Africa; and (2) slavery was a necessary evil because everyone knows that Negroes are inferior to whites.

The quarter was the racially segregated, and therefore deprived, neighborhood on the east side of Grapeland, just beyond a fence line at which all city amenities, such as power and water, stopped. Only black people lived in the quarter, where, without the benefit of electricity, water, or sewer lines, they subsisted in a stagnant form of poverty not all that dissimilar from what their ancestors had experienced in slavery.

In the days of the old plantation system, slaves resided in what was known as slave quarters, but in my childhood, that plural descriptor had been reduced to a singular noun that described every Southern town's Negro section. From Savannah to Richmond and all the way back to Houston, every Southern city along with every wide place in an unpaved red dirt road supported the evil institution of the quarter.

My earliest memories are of riding in an old Chevrolet with Uncle Will as he peddled in the quarter. "Peddling" was his term for selling produce and sweet milk, buttermilk, and the like to the black people who somehow clung to life year in and year out in tiny tar paper shacks that turned into ovens in summer and remained sufficiently cold on winter nights to cause their inhabitants to shiver under layers of hand-stitched quilts.

When I was young, I would remain in the front seat of the car and watch Uncle Will haggle with his customers over the price of whatever he had to peddle that day. By the time I'd finished second grade, I was allowed to stand next to him and watch up close as he traded milk for a handful of nickels, dimes, or, on occasion, dollar bills.

He never questioned the morality of having a quarter. I suspect the culture that reared him as what most at the tail end of the nineteenth century called "white trash" conditioned him to cope by not questioning but accepting. Nevertheless, what I remember most about my time in the quarter with Uncle Will was his integrity. Few, if any, of his customers could read or do simple math, yet this man never cheated a soul. He certainly could have, but he didn't. He kept a careful record of each sale, the majority of which were made on credit, but he never, not even one time, tweaked the numbers he kept recorded in a spiral notebook no wider than his hand. No doubt, his losses regularly exceeded his gains, but, just the same, he never cheated or inflated his prices. More times than I can remember, he climbed into the Chevrolet, shrugged, and said, "Well, I reckon I best forgive old So-and-So's debt."

Uncle Will went to his grave with many people owing him money. But in this life he never pressured anyone. He simply accepted two facts: life is unfair, and there is never a good reason to surrender your integrity to the devil that is greed.

—*Dad*

The Sand Hill

Dear Sarah,

WHEN I WAS A BOY, MY GRANDFATHER REGALED ME WITH STORIES OF his childhood adventures of hunting deer and even black bear in these very woods. But throughout the course of our hunting together, we had seen nothing bigger or more intriguing to fire my imagination than a plentiful supply of red squirrels, the rare bobcat, or a few coyotes that, on occasion, howled at night in the distance. The best either of us could report was an occasional cloven track much too small to be a calf. Still, we talked almost daily of our shared longing to spot a deer on the small piece of earth of which we had been made temporary stewards. We never did.

On a cold March day a little more than twenty years after my grandfather left this life, a doe bounded over the slack in the rusty barbed wire. I remained still atop the sand hill in a shallow rut a March rain had turned to cold mud the night before. The animal neither sniffed nor spied me as her nostrils studied the breeze. I knelt as if I were suddenly overwhelmed by the need to pray, and I watched her trot a ways cautiously, halt, and then meander up the muddy rise straight toward me, as though the two of us had agreed to meet on this early spring afternoon. Kneeling in the wet sand where my grandfather and I had plowed so many straight furrows behind our horses Old Nick and Nancy, I suddenly felt the warmth that drove him to love so freely and so fully.

The deer continued her delicate trek toward me. I whispered a string of inane encouragements as though she could hear me and might understand. Suddenly she stopped, not ten yards away. I remained motionless, and, without benefit of any of the five senses, I knew my grandfather was with me, atop the sand hill, his favorite place on our 168 acres, with me in a sacred, mystical moment that brought me to my knees in wet sand for reasons I could not begin to comprehend.

My whispers turned to a simple declaration of the obvious, "There's a deer. She's a doe, I reckon." The wind carried a question through a stand of pines, "Now ain't she pretty?"

"Yes, sir, and I'm so thankful that we finally got to see her together."

"Me, too," spoke the wind before departing and leaving me alone to admire the yearling doe for a moment more before she, too, abandoned me to memories mixed with wonderment, joy, and mystery atop the old sand hill.

—Dad

Chaos Theory

Dear Sarah,

A WOMAN CAME TO SEE ME THIS MORNING WHO HAS SEEMINGLY dedicated her life to chaos. She lives here, then there, always dreaming, scheming, and then streaking off in all directions at once.

She possesses a remarkable talent. She is a musician, but, tragically, she usually conceals her gift from the world by making chaos the vehicle through which she expresses herself. Chaos has become her primary defense. She doesn't live the poetry that is in her spirit. As bizarre as it sounds, she remains convinced that she keeps herself safe from an adversarial, even at times abusive, world by remaining frenetic, off-balance, and close to debilitated by a daily infusion of disorganization. And yet, when she sings, her words ring with such clarity that there can be little doubt their origin is inspired, their purpose is to heal.

The second she lays her six-string guitar into its battered case, tears betray a counterfeit little smile. It is then that I long to show her what is inside of her hammering for freedom against the nearly impregnable wall of fear she long ago erected. As he has done for all of us, God has made her only a little less than holiness and has crowned her with glory and honor.

I refrain from telling her this because to proclaim this truth would be to push much too hard against her defenses. This is something she must discover on her own because after all, it is truth's nature to be discovered. So, I sit with her each week and I listen, and following every session, I pray for her. And I attach to each of these petitions the hope that she may someday come to see that she is safe and that a soulful expression of love is not only her song, but, even more, her reason to be.

—Dad

Love in a Pancake House

Dear Sarah,

THE YOUNG WAITRESS IN WACO COULD NOT HAVE BEEN OLD ENOUGH to enroll as a freshman at Baylor University across the street; nevertheless, she was already a no-nonsense professional who knew her way around a dining room as she balanced more plates in one trip than most of us are called upon to tote in a week. I spotted her as I waited in a crowded hallway with my back pressed firmly against the wall. For no greater cause than spurning a boredom that has a way of sliding toward annoyance, I studied her and the other waitresses. In violation of Jesus' admonition not to judge anyone, I judged these women and their apparent efficiency.

Ten or so were hopping about quicker than autumn crickets. Some appeared sufficiently haggard to convince me that this was their last stop in a lifetime so riddled with heartache as to make the experience of living seem hardly worth the effort. Others, such as the pert dyed-blonde kid I selected as their champion, were obviously still fresh, brimming with hope, and scurrying about until something better came along or until the young men of their dreams galloped on white horses by this pancake house and slowed down only long enough to carry them away from fast food, feigned friendliness, and frenetic servitude.

Moments before my name was called into a microphone that didn't work, the cashier summoned to the phone the young woman I'd chosen grand champion. Obviously, these servants were not expected to receive personal calls, because the phone was located in the most inhospitable place I could imagine. The thing was attached to the wall next to where I sat, so I could hear almost every word that this young woman uttered.

I heard her ask expectantly, "For real?" Then the hope that had earlier shone in her face faded. She buried her face into the crook of her elbow, muffling her words. After she hung up, she turned to the cashier and revealed, "Oh, my God, my grandmother was in a wreck."

The cashier embraced her while the kid maintained a stoic composure. The older woman asked, "Are you okay?" The youngster smiled as she fought hard against the coming avalanche of worry. "I'm okay," she assured the woman before wriggling out of her embrace.

Another waitress suddenly appeared to inquire as to her welfare. Although obviously still stunned, the kid nodded and said in a voice loud enough for me to hear, "I'm okay." A third woman inquired of her well-being, then joined a fourth as she listened to the news. Within two minutes, she was again toting a pile of plates, but her eyes were glazed and her stare fixed. Other women approached her to hug her or merely to tap her on the shoulder as she passed by. Obviously, the word of her grandmother's accident had spread quickly through this humble sisterhood.

Moments later, I was seated, and the young woman offered what could best be described as confusion sitting atop what I suspected to be habitual indifference. Ordinarily, I would have felt irritated, but today I didn't. I only marveled at the young woman who was now frightened, yet getting on with her work, and at a dining room filled with females who seemed genuinely to care about one another in the midst of the chaos of simple capitalism.

As I later stepped into the parking lot, I passed a rough man about my own age wearing the rebel flag sown crudely into his grimy cap. I turned in time to see the woman whom only a half hour before I had voted champion pouring that day's tips into the man's grease-stained hands. Was this child the de facto head of some terribly dysfunctional clan of passive/dependent adults? Was this kid paying for a tow truck, or was it the admission fee to some hospital emergency room she was shelling out? Whatever it was, it was all she had, and like a poor widow in one of Jesus' stories, she gladly gave it all away.

The rough man roared away in a hundred-dollar car as this beautiful young child stood alone on the sidewalk, now penniless but seemingly even more determined not to cry. And I prayed for her and for her grandmother as she stepped back inside the small restaurant where I was certain of one thing: she was loved.

—Dad

Going to Hell with Jesus

Dear Sarah,

As I arrived at the ferry separating Lake Norfork from that morning's destination—a tiny Presbyterian church on the far shore—I glanced at my watch and grimaced. I was somewhere between panic and prayer when the ferryman, a gruff fellow whose sense of humor seemed to have been eroded by too many years in the sun, motioned for me to drive the Chevrolet onto his boat. I complied with a worried smile and decided against attempting a conversation. Within fifteen minutes, the bald tires of my old car were once more on the road to Gamaliel, Arkansas, a small burg named for a great Pharisee.

As I drove toward the only steeple I could see above the thick pine boughs, I spied two old men in ill-fitting suits who appeared worried. Both were sweating the proverbial bullets in the hot shade of a huge pine. They'd obviously been negotiating for some time, but neither of them was prepared to admit defeat. Rolling to a stop, I leaned through the car window to ask, "Can you direct me to the Presbyterian church?"

I sensed the spirit of both lifting as though a wind had caught the sails attached to their souls.

"Are you Reverend Lively?" one asked while the other gazed at me with expectant eyes.

"Guilty as charged," I answered.

"Thank the Lord!" the other declared, with eyes uplifted as though·God's home were in the pine bough above.

"Am I that late?" I inquired with new worry.

"No, you ain't late at all. But for the past hour, old Homer and me have been standing under this here tree scrapping over which one of us was going to have to preach in the event you didn't show."

"Well, I showed," I said, stepping out of the car and toward their place in the churchyard.

They led me into a study long ago abandoned when their pastor left this life. The church had so dwindled in membership it could no longer afford the services of a regular pastor. Hence, they were left to loan out their pulpit on a regular basis to the likes of me.

The gentleman named Homer lingered with me in the study while the other man dashed off, as fast as an old farmer can, to tend to some other kind of ecclesiastical business. After lifting a cup of stale, tepid coffee to my lips, I traded smiles with the sunburned old gentleman who remained. I intuited that he meant to share with me an issue he found difficult to impart.

I waited as the organ announced the processional. After some stammering, the old man managed to utter, "Mr. Lively, Jesus don't go to hell in this church."

"Okay," I responded as though I understood the man's meaning. I stepped through the door and into the sanctuary's antique chancel. Two men and one woman composed the choir, and all of them appeared old enough to remember the First World War. Somewhere between their first struggle with an anthem and the reading of Scripture, it dawned on me that what the man meant was that in the recitation of the Apostles' Creed, the congregation omitted the phrase "he descended into hell." I'd heard of this practice in other churches, but I'd never experienced this omission in any Presbyterian church. When the time arrived to say the creed, though, I omitted this phrase, to the obvious relief of the man who had earlier timidly made his request.

Before I left the church early that afternoon, the old man walked me to the Chevrolet, took my hand in his own, and thanked me profusely for not sending Jesus to hell.

Since that morning, I've never been requested to omit the phrase. But if I were, I would adamantly refuse, and I would do so on the grounds that I don't want to imagine any place where Jesus has not been. Jesus made the Psalter his prayer book and, no doubt, read and pondered the two questions in Psalm 139:7: "Where can I go from your spirit? Or where can I flee from your presence?"

By definition, hell is where God's presence is absent, and yet, it is even to this dark place that Jesus is willing to venture to find us and to bring us home. The meaning of this is so profound as to transcend the limits of our comprehension, for by Jesus' willingness to trust the Scriptures and go where we believe God cannot possibly be, God also goes. And wherever God goes, hell disappears. Consequently, every time Jesus descends into hell, to quote the creed, hell surrenders its shadows to the light and thereby ceases to be.

If there is any better news than the power of God and the illusory nature of hell, I fail to imagine what it might be.

—Dad

Honk If You Love Jesus

Dear Sarah,

I'D FINISHED PREACHING IN THE HILL COUNTRY CHURCH BUT HAD declined the generous offer of a free supper so that I might get a head start toward home. At the bottom of the first steep hill beyond the town limits marker, I drove into a dangerous predicament. The road signs warned against driving on the shoulder of this two-lane blacktop, yet the huge pickup behind me was threatening to run over me. The driver blinked his headlights and appeared ready to ram the rusty bumper of my aging Toyota. I downshifted into fourth to gain traction on the incline, only to be blinded once more by the impatient driver's high beams firing off and on and reflecting in the rearview mirror.

"Patience," I screamed to no avail through the open front window. Once more the driver behind me blinked and honked, and this time I offered to the coming night an expletive that was, fortunately, lost in the wind. The blinking and honking continued without pause until I crested the hill. In violation of official edicts, I pulled to the shoulder, thus allowing the insufferable driver of the pickup to pass.

As the truck roared past, filling the night with diesel fumes, I spied a sticker affixed to its bumper. It offered what I considered an odd invitation, considering the circumstances: "Honk if you love Jesus."

Now, as best I know how, I do, in fact, love Jesus and all that he stood for and all that his eternal and holy spirit is about today. Nevertheless, on that Texas Hill Country evening, I decided against complying with the invitation for fear the driver of this truck would force me to the side of the road and assault me right there.

135

Whoever the driver was, he came precariously close to injuring or, worse yet, killing me. The way I see it, the fellow behind the wheel of that pickup was either driving someone else's vehicle or he stands in prodigious need of being born again—again.

—Dad

Coach

Dear Sarah,

MY SOFTBALL COACH WAS ONE OF THE GREAT MEN OF MY CHILDHOOD. He was a devoted husband, the father of three beautiful daughters, an officer in the church that raised me, and the perennial coach of our softball team. Every time I watched my idol, and the team's star pitcher, Tommy, who was four years my senior, strike out one batter after another with a windmill pitch that seemed fast enough to race a bullet and sometimes win, I longed to pitch for this man.

As a result of this ache in my heart, I would stand for hours and windmill a beat-up softball against the brick wall of our garage until it felt as though my arm might drop off. But unlike the legendary Tommy, for whom pitching a strike seemed as natural as spitting, my pitches flew on occasion high enough to threaten a mockingbird and into the dirt so often that by that season's end our backyard resembled a prairie dog town.

Nevertheless, I decided that success lay with practice, and by the time I had reached my thirteenth birthday, I was satisfied that my strikes against the garage wall were every bit as frequent as my wild pitches. Hence, it was time to try out for pitcher on the team. And since my idol Tommy had matriculated to grander opportunities in our small world of summer softball, our team was in need of an infusion of new blood. As best I could read the signs, I was to be "the man."

My tryout went better than expected, with strikes flying over home plate with such regularity as to make me embrace as truth the Presbyterian doctrine of predestination. On that cold March afternoon, nothing could have been more obvious than the fact that I had been predestined by the Almighty to be the next Tommy. In my mind, there could be no higher honor, and I was more than prepared to accept my status as living softball legend.

The first and only full inning I ever pitched went well enough. I struck out two batters, and the third popped out on an infield fly. I felt so confident that, as I swaggered toward the dugout, I spit a couple of wads of bubble gum juice into the red dirt, just as I had witnessed Tommy do countless times.

The next inning, however, was a much different story. The opposing coach read me like I was his family's Bible. His experienced eye pierced my thin armor and discerned a flaw waiting to be exposed. The man called time-out and whispered to his first hitter. These guys were up to something. Fear gripped my arm, causing my next pitch to sail like a flushed bobwhite over the wire mesh backstop. I could hear the laughter and even a few jeers coming from the crowd. Suddenly I could not buy a strike. With tears making my vision suddenly opaque, I focused as hard as I knew how to convince myself that I was once more in the backyard and hurling my familiar, mushy, worn-out ball at the garage. But nothing worked and, following every four pitches, another batter advanced to first base.

I hung my head as our beloved coach approached me slowly and with such agony that I saw that my failure had become his burden. He placed his strong arms about my sore, skinny shoulders as I wept. Only slightly above a whisper, he said, "Bobby, I love you, but you can't pitch for me anymore tonight."

Twenty-eight years later, I was to learn that this good man had departed this life. Almost exactly a year after hearing this sad news, I was invited by his wife and three daughters to officiate at an informal memorial service.

On a warm spring afternoon, his family gathered in a field in the small and mostly dead town of Venus, Texas, where, as a boy, my former coach loved to fly kites. I read a few words from the Bible that I had been told were meaningful to him, and then I listened as, one by one, a circle of friends and family spoke of this man's mission of expressing kindness in every situation. Following this tearful sharing, his wife dug a shallow hole in the loose, black dirt with her bare hands, and into it she poured his ashes.

Still on her knees, this woman suddenly looked up at me with eyes so filled with expectation that I could find no words to utter. I honestly didn't know what to do or say, so I simply stepped forward and extended my hand to my former coach's wife. She allowed me to pull her gently to her feet. And I found the strength to share my own story of a man who taught me in my thirteenth year that love is truth, and truth often means making the tough choices love requires.

—Dad

Born Again

Dear Sarah,

I DON'T BELIEVE IT WHEN ANYONE TELLS ME THAT THEY ARE BORN again, and that is because every such declaration is nothing more than an expression of pride.

Being born again is a matter of becoming conscious. Once someone has been born again, the ego is so surrendered to the Spirit that all need for boasting and other expressions of pride evaporate. Therefore, the born-again Christian would never think to tell someone that he or she had been blessed with the gift of consciousness.

Conscious human beings, on the one hand, embrace and even choose humbly to live a conviction that the expression of love is always more important than defending or promoting pride's agenda. Consequently, conscious people allow their lives gradually to become the instruments of God's will, which means they seldom point to themselves or to their accomplishments in the process of their spiritual growth.

Religious human beings, on the other hand, are fond of categories and all too often short on consciousness. They tend to view the church as simply one more arena for competition, where Brother So-and-So or Sister Saint is better than or worse than someone else.

I even once heard of a carpool of born-again mothers in an exclusive section of Dallas. It seems that before one of these women could become eligible to drive other people's children to school or soccer practice or the like, she was required to sign a pledge that she was a born-again Christian. This is a sad demonstration of precisely what being born again is not.

Recently, I met a former prison inmate in Austin who has

devoted his life since getting out of prison to expressing love. He earned a college degree and even achieved the credential of licensed drug and alcohol counselor with the State of Texas. His spiritual journey has so affected him that his ego has diminished and his spirit has caught fire with a genuine and generous compassion. Today this recovering man makes it possible for other addicted men and women to enjoy a place to live and to find and hold on to meaningful employment once they are released from prison.

During a conversation with me, he described in vivid detail the hardships facing those he attempts to help. He never one time mentioned himself or praised himself or in any way sought to make himself out a hero. He simply mentioned the difficulties and then spoke in reverence of small victories for which he assigned the glory to God. This is what I have come to believe it means to be "born again."

Many people have become conscious (read "born again"), but we seem to know very little about them. The reason is that those who are conscious have no need to seek the limelight. Nevertheless, they are the glue that holds this unconscious world together.

—Dad

Answered Prayer

Dear Sarah,

A NEWBORN AFRICAN ANTELOPE LAY ABANDONED AND HELPLESS IN A Texas pasture for reasons concealed from my awareness. Unexpected sadness draped itself about me like a shroud as I glimpsed the frail animal's fight to stand. In the rearview mirror I witnessed it struggling to right herself, all to no avail. "God," I whispered, as though this spontaneous utterance might suffice as a prayer powerful enough to prolong the life of innocence. Before I could make sense out of the small unfolding drama, I drove over the hill. I promised myself to revisit this tragic scene up close if the creature was still there upon my return trip.

Miles away I decided that I could not think about nature as tragedy, because such thoughts only bring me down when I work so hard to get up and to stay up emotionally. Nevertheless, tears welled in my eyes as I assured myself that my thoughts were now somewhere between silly and absurd.

I bought the newspaper I'd driven to town to read and sighed as I realized that, once more, my editor had improved my latest attempt at a column. I bought a friend a cup of coffee and joked with a couple who, for that moment, shared the same coffee shop with me and the kid behind the counter. I then headed back toward the meadow, where I hoped, in fact, prayed, that I might find the antelope gone.

To my astonishment, the February grass that stretched before me was now filled with children, most of whom were running about and squealing as they joined in making airborne a small force of bright paper kites. It was as though the old woman who lived in a shoe had liberated her many children to spend the warm Hill Country afternoon playing upon a still-dormant winter meadow.

I prayed before I slowed the car and, as much to my relief as to my amazement, I discovered the antelope gone. What had come to replace the death struggle was sheer joy riding on the sounds of a valley filled with beautiful children. "Thank you!" I whispered, and in a little girl's distant squeal I imagined I could hear God say, "You're most welcome!"

—Dad

A Thin Place

Dear Sarah,

I FIRST VISITED MO-RANCH IN THE SUMMER OF 1949. THE Presbyterians had recently purchased this magnificent ranch just west of Hunt from the estate of Dan Moran, who, at his untimely death, served as the president of Conoco Oil. This man was a visionary whose dreams for a one-of-a-kind Texas Hill Country hacienda fortunately did not outstrip either his considerable resources or his passion for establishing something unique on the banks of the Guadalupe River. His dream later became one of the premier conference centers in this country.

By the time I reached my fourth birthday, I was told every Sunday that I, along with every other Presbyterian in Texas, was now the proud, though partial, owner of a ranch. No news could have delighted me more. Therefore, the summer before that challenge otherwise known as kindergarten, I joined my mother and father and older brother Bill in making the arduous, not to mention unair-conditioned, trek down a two-lane blacktop all the way from Dallas to Mo-Ranch. I was scarcely old enough to translate experience into memories, but I will never forget this long day's journey into my personal destiny.

In the summer of 1963, I returned to Mo-Ranch and worked in the cafeteria. And it was in that unforgettable season that I was introduced to the faculty of Austin Presbyterian Theological Seminary. Never before had I witnessed so many brilliant and interesting human beings sitting on one porch. I knew little except that I wanted to be as much like these distinguished ladies and gentlemen as possible. If attending seminary proved crucial to such a transformation, then so be it, I thought.

Ever since my initial visit to the banks of the North Fork of the Guadalupe, Mo-Ranch has continued to play an important role in my life. In fact, I was there not long ago leading a spiritual retreat when it dawned on me that this place was created by God and made inviting by a visionary so that ordinary folks like me might come to know what it means to experience what I have learned to call a "thin place."

What exactly is a thin place? It's anyplace in the present tense in which the membrane separating the Spirit realm and the material world has been worn thin by earnest and sincere prayer. I am aware of few such places on earth, but I am convinced that Mo-Ranch is one of them. No icons weep by streams of water, and no holy apparitions appear; nevertheless, the ground here is hallowed, and the silence that fills the canyon is rife with a profundity that sometimes speaks of solace even to the most tortured soul.

As I walked beneath the canopy of stars high above Mo-Ranch last week, I listened hard between the memories for some new and passionate mandate or for some whispered hint of a future beyond the disease that resides in my heart or for some subtle correction to the path I have followed for the last few years. Self-antagonistic distractions interfered with my concentration. I longed to cry, and yet I was sufficiently cogent to recognize that sincere, perhaps even cathartic, prayer was screaming to be expressed.

But the word required for honest prayer would in no way attach itself to any present reality. "Denial," I mumbled to the starry night in a sudden wince, as the sweet Guadalupe spilled over the dam on its gentle way to the sea.

Later I lay awake and considered prayers I couldn't muster the courage to express. And the night at this thin place spoke to me of the identical reassurances she had deigned to utter when I was but a small child. I smiled as I felt grace hold me in her arms. Confession seemed the only sane response for a life marked by undeserved blessings, but I chose instead to rest once more in the glorious silence. And when sleep arrived to rob me of the resolve to hear the further nuances of mystery on that winter night, I managed simple words of gratitude for gifts I no more understood than I did back in 1949.

Hours later, the sun lifted her radiance above limestone to erase the shadows cast both by a cold night and fear. I basked in the glory of it all—of a love that will not give up, no matter what, of sins not only forgiven but forgotten, of a hope as fresh as a new Hill Country morning, and of a love so amazing that it discourages description and so redemptive that even the most shattered life can recover its center.

This knowing happens other places, I suspect, for love is in no way restricted by either our loyalties or our self-centered perceptions. Nevertheless, for reasons that must necessarily remain hidden, there exists a place in the Texas Hill Country where springs pour out of the stone and where hills rise to swap secrets with the sky.

For the past fifty years, the Presbyterians have called Mo-Ranch home, but I know this narrow, winding valley as a thin place. It is here that God speaks in breezes raking the river and in a love so silent and so determined that it penetrates the walls of even our best defenses.

—Dad

Holding a Newborn

Dear Sarah,

THIS BABY WAS BUT ONE WEEK OLD THE DAY I MET HER. A YOUNG couple had adopted her on the very day I had been invited to speak in the church to which they belonged. And when I say "belonged," I mean they really belonged. As I stood in the fellowship hall of that benevolent community, I smiled as I watched one person after another take the child and hold her and then declare to the rest of the gathering crowd the indisputable truth of this little girl's beauty. Her eyes were the hue of coal and matched perfectly a cluster of hair sprigs waiting to turn into a soft and lovely frame for a face destined to charm.

I rejoiced in being glad in this baby's safe arrival in this world, but I also found myself wondering about the mother, who, for whatever reason, was compelled to give up one so exquisite. I couldn't imagine what drove her to such a decision save righteousness. How did this mother's life become so difficult that she could not keep her own child? I wondered regarding the details or the emotional consequence of such a decision. Nevertheless, I prayed for this mother as I grinned at the little one and even more at the women in the church who almost came to blows over the privilege of holding one so fine.

Then I wondered what this world might be like if all of us could learn to love ourselves with the same passion I envisaged in the women who held that child. If we were to do that, everything would be changed and so different that never again would any child go begging for nurture. What I witnessed in those women holding that newborn was a glimpse of the future grounded in the present tense or, more precisely, what our Lord might have meant when he said, "On earth as it is in heaven." And in heaven's presence, I rejoiced. I always do.

—Dad

Happy Birthday

Dear Sarah,

TODAY IS YOUR BIRTHDAY. IT WAS ALMOST THREE DECADES AGO THIS morning that an Arkansas doctor drove in during an ice storm to deliver you. I heard you cry, and then he handed you to me and said, "Allow me to introduce you to your daughter."

Once I returned your wet, wiggling body to his gentle care, I turned and scribbled a poem on the back of the checkbook register. In it I promised I would never abandon you. For three decades now I've gladly kept the vow I swore to you on the morning of your birth. I've been there every day of your life, in the triumphs and in the disappointments, and through it all I have loved you quite imperfectly. And in every circumstance, both you and God have forgiven me for the mistakes I made in assisting your wonderful mother in rearing you.

I am now sufficiently wise to extend the vow I made to you so long ago. Actually, I'm not extending it at all. By its very content, the thing is extending itself because since your birth, I have discovered that love is forever. Everything else will come to an end, even the universe, I am told, but not love, because love is who God is, and God is eternal.

My life will come to an end someday, perhaps even quite soon. I really don't know how sick I am, but I am told my heart is very weak. I suspect, however, that I do have some time remaining to enjoy seeing you grow into who your Creator has in mind for you to become. And as I wrote to you at the beginning of these letters, I hope to live long enough to see the bluebonnets bloom in the Texas Hill Country one more time.

In truth, there are days when I think of the very real possibility of an early departure, and I am saddened by the thought of being separated from you. But I want you to know this: wherever I go, in this life or beyond its finite boundaries, my love for you will always be. And once I am privileged to be with God, I will love you even more than I do today simply because I will be reunited with Love, who is inexplicably our Source and simultaneously our Destiny.

I'm so thankful that you came into this world because you, more than anyone else, have taught me well that the single reason any of us is here is to love. So happy birthday, my precious daughter, and may you be given many, many more to celebrate.

I love you.

—Dad

Expressing Love

Dear Sarah,

SAINT JOHN OF THE CROSS TELLS US THAT WE CANNOT KNOW GOD save by love. This idea works since we know by Scripture that God is love. Love, then, is the way to God, and this makes sense because how else could we know something except by participating in its essence? For example, how can we expect to be a part of a river unless we first jump in?

God is not thought; therefore, no cognitive construct, no matter how eloquent and sophisticated, will prove sufficient when it comes to appropriating the essence of God. This idea disappoints the theologians I've known and studied under in the past, but their negative reaction in no way obviates the certitude that God can only be known by love. Besides, I've known theologians who, at least in my perspective, appear to find it difficult to love their students and, perhaps, anyone with the disciplines of kindness and compassion. Some I have known were even somewhere between mean and ornery all the while they professed to be teaching about God.

Some years ago, the church that holds my ordination developed an aphorism it embossed on letterheads and affixed with adhesive to rear bumpers of trucks and cars. It read, "Theology Matters!" The only problem with this so-called truth, which is a passionate issue for some, is that theology is knowledge. And as Paul so bluntly put it in his initial letter to the Church at Corinth, knowledge passes away while "love never ends."

Theology's greatest danger is to be found in the fact that few people can really read it and absorb it. If you don't believe me, invite any layman to read any volume of Barth's *Church*

Dogmatics and walk away from the experience edified. The consequence of this is that theology's very existence can, if we are not very careful, support an ecclesiastical elitism. This particular ugliness presents itself as an arrogance wherein the "trained" are quick to inform the rest of us that they are better able to "think" about God and, therefore, to know God than are the great untrained masses.

But Jesus taught us that to receive his kingdom was to be like children in the sense of being open and eager to learn. I once invited a noted theologian to the church I was serving at the time. Hundreds gathered to hear what this learned doctor had to say. After my glowing introduction of him, he paused and made this stunning (not to mention arrogant) declaration: "If you cannot read Greek, you cannot possibly understand the New Testament!" Suddenly, everyone in that lecture hall, including me, was disenfranchised from the New Testament.

Later that same summer, I preached in a small country church in East Texas. Following the service, a farm family invited me to their humble house, where they served me a sumptuous meal of homegrown foods. I remember the man telling me how much he enjoyed reading the New Testament, although he felt inadequate to do so with no more than a grammar-school education. Yet this man, unlike the theologian mentioned above, knew what it meant to love. In fact, for him the expression of love seemed as natural as turning the ground behind his two big Molly mules in the first days of spring. Over the years, his life had so become the incarnation of love that it was obvious that his life reflected God. This is the very best any of us can hope for simply because Saint John of the Cross was right: love is the only way to God.

The Power of Love

Dear Sarah,

THE CARDIOLOGIST CALLED TO SAY THAT THE FIRST DIAGNOSTIC TEST since the advent of my illness indicated that I would likely beat this disease. Apparently, this is not a common occurrence in the course of congestive heart failure. At first, I was joyfully stunned to hear him proclaim in his soft, Southern drawl the good, even dramatic, news. After hanging up, I picked up my puppy and declared to her, "I'm going to live!" She responded by licking my nose.

About a week before this long-scheduled test, I accepted an invitation to speak at St. Matthew's Episcopal Church in Austin. Following the talk I delivered on the need for healing the rift within us, I stepped down from the pulpit and was greeted by several members of that fine congregation.

After several minutes of sharing, I happened to notice a diminutive woman clutching a Bible so close to her as to cause me to wonder regarding her emotional well-being. My thinking began to race the way it does whenever I scan my memory bank for names. All that I could recall was the name Sandy and the fact that long ago she and I had been in a small group together and that she had written me letters off and on over the course of a decade.

Her letters were as racked with pain as they were infrequent, but each thanked me for some small bit of hope she'd discovered in my newspaper column. As best I could recall, I responded to each letter with nothing more than an obligatory and brief word of gratitude. And now she stood obviously waiting to have a word with me as she clutched her Bible. She appeared as though afraid someone might yank it from her.

More memories surfaced. I recalled that she had been horrifically abused as a little girl. Not surprising, the result of this abuse had been a crippling case of chronic anxiety and the ineffectual and equally painful defense of reclusion.

But somewhere in what must have been one lonely year after another, grace gave birth within her soul to courage, and she finally asked for help. Her healing began the day she dared to push against her daunting fear and walked into a therapist's office. And it was sometime during the course of her work with this compassionate physician that she decided to write to me.

Armed with nothing more than this sketchy information and her first name, I approached her with a smile. She offered a similar grin and said, "I know you are sick." Her possession of this information did not surprise me, because I'd written of my disease in more than one column. But what she said next caught me off guard. She asked, "May I pray for you?" I responded, "Well, yeah, sure."

What she did next initially embarrassed me. She tucked her Bible under her arm and placd her hand on my forehead. Without further warning, she began to pray, asking God to heal me.

My reaction was strong; I wanted out. I regularly avoid being the center of any kind of attention. I worried that the two of us might be "grandstanding" for Jesus as we stood together in a sanctuary praying.

After the first few words flowed from her gentle spirit, an unexpected warmth coursed through my being. And as she beseeched the Holy Spirit to restore me to health, I wondered on the far side of my initial burst of discomfort if what I was feeling was a manifestation of divine healing or, perhaps, a somatic reaction to subliminal suggestion.

She uttered an "amen" and the warmth dissipated. I thanked her, offered her a farewell hug, and strolled into the cold February evening uncertain of what had transpired between us. I'm far too rational and much too fond of empiricism, I told myself, to believe in this woman's kind of unabashed intercession.

Five days later, my doctor, who is one of this nation's most respected cardiologists, called to report that the results from my echocardiogram were in his words, "covered with grace." I would likely fully recover from what six months ago had been described to me as a progressive and deadly disease.

I've long taught of Jesus healing the sick and giving sight to the blind. And yet, in the wake of my own unexpected healing, I discovered that my biggest problem is not with my heart at all. No, my problem lies in my blindness, which is to say, in my trenchant unwillingness to see the power of love to heal even an overeducated, highly skeptical old hypocrite like me.

—Dad

Waiting for Bluebonnets

Dear Sarah,

I PERCHED UPON A PICNIC TABLE YESTERDAY AS THE BLUSTER OF March rattled the bare hackberry limbs above me. The wind turned to rake the Pedernales River before sailing off toward Mexico. I smiled as I recognized the remnants of the half bag of peanuts I'd poured upon this same ground two weeks before.

Miles away, across a Texas lake, the phone I most often answer when I'm in the office was ringing, and the voice mail was recording the pleas and typically polite requests for assistance. Below, the river flowed as gracefully as a hydroelectric dam will allow. Behind me, a meadow of dormant buffalo clover waited for warmth, light, and the necessary nudge from God to explode into the magnificence of bluebonnets.

I longed to be invigorated by the wild, sweet fragrance of the temporary little flower that fills this canyon each spring, but yesterday was not the moment. And therein lies the lesson. The ancient Greeks called the appropriate time the *kairos*, which means a long-awaited moment is now at hand. But alone upon the picnic table, I admitted that although the wind was still cold and March insisted upon roaring like a lion for a while longer, the *kairos* was not now. It would be when the time was right, but this day was not it.

I gazed into the water's murkiness as I whispered a prayer beseeching God to grant me the courage simply to be, to settle easily in this present, and to trust, even though in that moment I was cold, brimming with questions, weighed down by worry, and severely scarred by resentment.

"Let me be content," I begged again. Riding on winter's

breath, holy words blew through me and paused only long enough to whisper to me of patience. I pledged my best intentions before the wind could carry them away. And once more, I turned toward the drab dormancy waiting for the *kairos*.

—Dad

A Corpse

Dear Sarah,

A FORMER PROFESSOR RECENTLY REFERRED AN UNUSUALLY YOUNG couple to my care. My counseling practice is by necessity a small, unheralded, and not-for-fee enterprise. The young wife called me and referred to my sagacious old friend, so I agreed to work these people into my schedule.

They both arrived on time, but separately. Their promptness pleased me, but my heart sank when I read the tension they dragged behind them like a heavy bag of ripe barnyard fertilizer.

These people reported that they had been married a bit more than three months and were already at war. I listened in sadness as they played the zero-sum game of he did/she did. Finally, I interrupted their bout of blame-throwing with this announcement: "This is not a marriage! This is a corpse!"

A hush came over them and me, too, as I surprised even myself with this sudden outburst of frustrated bluntness. I quietly invited them to seek individual therapy with the hope of discovering why it was that they were projecting such destructive and unconscious vitriol onto each other. I gave them each a recommendation for individual therapy and bade them a not-so-fond farewell.

What I would find fascinating if it were not so sad is that each week, one of them calls and then comes close to pleading with me to see them again as a couple. Each time I refuse because what they are up to, without even knowing it, is begging me to fix their marriage. The truth is that neither I nor any other human being can fix their relationship. Until they are influenced sufficiently by the pain they inflict upon themselves, they will go right on blaming each other, wounding each other, and calling the police on each other until they end up despising each other.

The most loving response I can make to people who are not sufficiently conscious enough to love is to stay out of their way until they discover that this life is not about winning, but about collaborating with heaven in the cause of allowing their individual lives to become compassion. Only holiness can bring them to this place. As for me, I can do little except pray for them to come to know what it means to love God, themselves, and each other in that order.

Abuse

Dear Sarah,

WHAT A BIZARRE THURSDAY THIS HAS BEEN! HAD I KNOWN WHAT was coming, I might never have climbed out of bed.

In today's mail I received a typed postcard bearing no name or return address. Whoever wrote this card characterized me as a con artist. Something I'd written a month ago in my column about seeking truth in seminary while I hid from the Vietnam War apparently pushed a button in a writer who would not sign his or her name.

I found my reaction upon seeing myself characterized as a con artist interesting. First, I felt inexplicably embarrassed. An aftershock of shame provided yet another blow. I thought, *I wonder if I am a con artist? Have I been hiding this from myself all these years?*

By the time I returned to my office and tossed the anonymous postcard where it belonged—in the trash—I confessed once more that I'm a sinner and even an avowed hypocrite. But a con artist? No, I'm not a con artist. But I am, without question, a man who stands in need of the same grace the individual needs who wrote that card and mailed it anonymously.

I decided not to let the characterization trouble me, because the only issue of any real importance is what God thinks of me. I know God loves me, sins and all, and what the writer of the postcard thinks of me is none of my business. Still, I must pray for him or her and remember once more that people who have not experienced the miracle of transformation project their personal pain onto the rest of us.

—Dad

Meekness

Dear Sarah,

EVERY TIME I PASS HIS SON'S DENTAL OFFICE IN A SMALL HILL Country town not far from Austin, I think of my high school coach. He graduated from Baylor University after earning more than one letter in football and came to Dallas to coach. I was fortunate to know him as a high school history teacher, coach, friend, and fellow Presbyterian. He and his family belonged to the same church where my mom and dad were members and where I'd taken communion since my ninth birthday.

He was always kind and extraordinarily interested in me. When he spotted me sitting with my buddies in the school lunchroom, he smiled, nodded, and, occasionally, paused long enough to pat me on the shoulder and say something like, "You're going to do well in life."

Years later, when I had become sufficiently mature to regard meekness as a hard-earned virtue, I would think of this man. He possessed enormous physical strength, impeccable character, and yet an almost feminine gentleness. And it was this last quality that made him memorable, at least in my view.

One spring afternoon not far from the date I was scheduled to graduate from high school, a buddy of mine shocked all of us by suddenly standing up in the lunchroom and hurling a half-eaten apple across a dozen tables to smash against the back of Coach's head. The thing exploded like a grenade. Coach turned slowly to see every student in that room staring silently at the linoleum floor. I lifted my gaze only enough to see him wiping the remains of the apple from his head and neck with his handkerchief before he began walking slowly toward where I sat.

I glimpsed his slight, enigmatic smile before I once more averted my gaze. He squeezed my shoulder gently and said, "Bobby, you know who threw that apple, don't you, son?" I nodded that I did. I remember hearing a wheezy sigh before he spoke again. "And I know you didn't do it." This time I wagged my head back and forth persuasively in the sure direction of no. Another sigh preceded this amazing proclamation of wisdom. "Well, I wasn't born with eyes in the back of my head, so I guess I'll never know who hit me. And I know you well enough to say that if I asked you, you'd tell me. But it would not be at all right to put you in that position. So I will never ask you that question." With that, he walked off, obviously embarrassed, no doubt livid, but determined to remain gentle.

This man was blessed because he decided to follow his Lord into a life of meekness, which is always the same thing—the strength to put love before the expression of one's true feelings. And it was this quality that, in that awful moment, saved my hide.

—Dad

Palm Sunday

Dear Sarah,

PALM SUNDAY IS NEXT WEEK. THE GOSPELS TELL OF JESUS RIDING into Jerusalem on the back of a young donkey and causing throngs of onlookers to line his parade route and wave palm fronds in exclamations of praise that included characterizing him as the son of Israel's greatest king. His feet must have come close to dragging the ground as he rode into a city on fire with the celebration of Passover. And he must have resembled a comedic parody of royalty far more than he reminded anyone of a conquering Caesar.

Scripture teaches us that Jesus made his entrance in this way to fulfill a prophecy contained in Zechariah 9:9:

> Rejoice greatly, O daughter Zion!
> Shout aloud, O daughter Jerusalem!
> Lo, your king comes to you;
> triumphant and victorious is he,
> humble and riding on a donkey,
> on a colt, the foal of a donkey.

But this prophecy kicks up as many questions as it answers. Foremost among them is this: Why did Jesus choose to live out this oracle and thereby make such an obviously humble entrance when he could just as easily have walked into Jerusalem and spared himself the embarrassment of becoming a public spectacle?

The answer is best expressed in this one word: obedience. In making this entrance, Jesus was proclaiming what today is termed a "meta-message" or, in other words, a small message about a larger message. Jesus' small message was this: I am absolutely willing to be who my Father would have me be; therefore, I am surrendered even if what I do appears foolish to the world. His larger message was that the realm of which he had been crowned king was a radically new, inverted society in which the first are last, the last first, the humble exalted, the exalted humbled; in which those who would be great descend into the lowly status of servant; in which those who seek self-aggrandizement remain frustrated; in which love is the only real power; and in which the king of all kings rides humbly on the back of a baby donkey.

Fishing at Bettye's

Dear Sarah,

YESTERDAY I JOINED TWO SAINTS IN TAKING A COUPLE OF FIFTEEN-year-olds fishing on a stock tank in East Texas. One saint is a youth minister and fishing expert; the other is a court-appointed special advocate for one of the young men.

Both kids are brimming with obvious potential. And yet both also hold in common two tragic circumstances: neither knows the identity of his father; and, early in life, both were abandoned. The demonic force driving a fateful wedge between two mothers and these beautiful sons was the disease of addiction.

I once heard a priest say that the first thing to go when one becomes addicted is the capacity to love. I've come to see this in the many people I have guided toward treatment. And because two women I will never meet succumbed to a disease determined to destroy the human spirit, I stood yesterday on the muddy banks of a stock tank in a light rain and admired from a distance two young men who have no parent to love them or guide them or praise them or forgive them. What they do have is the state, and what is the state but a tangle of regulations driven by a bureaucracy that all too often omits love from the equation.

I smiled as I remembered Bettye, who, since her husband died, has been the faithful steward of this land and this lake. No one I've ever met seems to know more about how to love than Bettye except, perhaps, the youth minister and the court-appointed special advocate.

Bettye once told me that if you can't sort things out fishing, then they probably can't be sorted out. Yesterday I did far more sorting than any real fishing; as a consequence, I took away far more hope than fish.

—Dad

Lifting My Eyes

Dear Sarah,

"I LIFT UP MY EYES TO THE HILLS" IS ONE OF THE MOST BEAUTIFUL but misunderstood passages in the whole of the Bible. This is also the first text I ever chose for a sermon.

I was invited to preach before several hundred children in an outdoor chapel that faced a panoramic view of the Mummy Range of the Colorado Rockies. As any biblically illiterate preacher might do, I totally misinterpreted the text and thereby made it say what it was never intended to proclaim. My point was this: when we look at the hills, we are reminded of the transcendent nature of God.

But the psalmist's reason for writing this ancient hymn of praise was to remind all people in every age that we are not to look to the hills, but only to God. And why are we not to look to the hills? Because in the hills surrounding Jerusalem, people had constructed altars to Baal. These so-called high places were shrines where men paid a priest a handsome fee for the privilege of enjoying sexual intercourse with a cultic prostitute in the cause of guaranteeing the birth of a son, a bumper crop, or some other blessing. This practice was an abomination to God and thus inspired the psalmist and others, such as the prophet Hosea, to rail against it.

I was amused a week or so back when a Christian association invited me to teach at its annual singles' conference. The organizers even mailed me a mock-up brochure that featured my name and the title of my course on a prominent page. And what was the theme of this year's conference? "I will lift my eyes to the hills." I laughed out loud before I wondered how often we mangle the truth with the snap judgments that fire our passionate errors.

—Dad

Doctor's Orders

Dear Sarah,

WHEN I WAS A KID, MY FAMILY OFTEN WENT TO THE MOUNTAINS IN Colorado. I would go off and sit for hours, until my parents came searching for me. I enjoyed watching the high peaks change moods in reaction to the whims of clouds. Each morning, before the clouds had time to gather in the Colorado sky to plot their day's course, I would glance at the Front Range only long enough to see its snowy peaks standing proud, even touching the sky, as my father was fond of saying, and always beautiful. Afternoon was much different, for it was then the drama arrived, replete with a thunder that shook whole valleys in the wake of tongues sufficiently fiery to remind me of the Bible's description of Pentecost. Following bursts of fury, wave upon wave of cold rain would arrive to baptize me as thick clouds cast a pall above the timberline.

I wrote my first poem when I was twelve, and, of course, the topic was my adoration of mountains. I dared not write of my love of a girl because of the insufferable teasing I would have experienced at the hands of three brothers and numerous buddies. But the assignment in seventh-grade English was to wax poetically of love, and so I did just that, and I did it in probably less than five minutes.

In that forgettable first effort, I characterized the Rockies as great ladies reaching toward the sky, and for the rest of my life I would greet them as such each time I was privileged to glimpse them, even from the window of an airplane. "Good morning, ladies," I would whisper so no one could hear me and think me insanely romantic.

If I were assigned the same task today, however, I fear sadness would likely interrupt the effort. The cardiologist informed me only a few days ago that I will never again return to the High Country. In disbelief, I pressed him, but he literally looked down his nose at me and warned, "If you go there, the altitude could kill you." So I won't go, but, oh, how I will miss them.

I only actually lived in the mountains for a few summers during my college years, but I always planned to return to them in my retirement. They were always "out there" just west of the horizon, waiting for me.

Biblical literalists might be so bold as to attempt to convince me that sin is the cause of what they would characterize as an expression of divine punishment. And they might even be so brazen as to use Moses to illustrate their point. After all, they might argue, Moses demonstrated sufficient pride to be disallowed entrance into the promised land.

I'm not being punished. There can be no question that I'm a sinner, but there is no punishment whatsoever in God. We punish ourselves, though, every time we step beyond the bounds of God's will, but disease just happens. It is never punishment.

—Dad

The Light Shines

Dear Sarah,

YOU AND I BOTH SO ENJOYED JACKSON, OUR AFFABLE OLD ENGLISH bulldog. Many of my happiest memories are connected to the countless afternoons I walked him a slow mile or so in the inner-city neighborhood of Dallas we called home.

No new house had been constructed anywhere within a several-mile radius of us for more than fifty years, so I was surprised one September morning to see a foundation being laid in a vacant lot. I enjoyed measuring the progress being made on this new house each day as Jackson and I sauntered by.

By early spring, the house was completed. From the bicycles lying about in the drive and the light shining through what I suspected was a kitchen window, I discerned the arrival of this home's first family. As I walked past, I whispered a prayer for them and gave them no more thought that day.

Several days later, I was stunned to see what looked from a distance to be a for sale sign driven into the spring mud. What could this mean? What could have gone so wrong that the family who built this home over the winter was abandoning it before the school year was finished? I hurried an always-ponderous bulldog as though a real-estate sign might provide answers. I was disturbed to discover that what stood before me in the twilight's glow was not a real-estate sign, but a homemade placard bearing the following warning:

> I have a gun!
> And I will shoot to kill whomever
> is stealing my new shrubs!

Jackson urinated on the signpost as, in disbelief, I read these words over and over again. I couldn't get away fast enough for fear the author of this threat would think me a thief and shoot me along with my lovable dog.

Several days later, I wandered past the house at a safe distance and paused only long enough to see that a lined page ripped from a spiral notebook had been tacked to the sign. Whoever left this note penned these unforgettable words:

> Please don't kill anyone!
> If someone steals your shrubs, call me.
> I will pay for their full replacement.

Below this appeal was a local phone number.

I walked away certain that I witnessed to the very top the meaning in John's words when he bequeathed to the ages this hopeful proclamation: "What has come into being in him was life, and the life was the light of all people" (John 1:4). And I rejoiced all the way home, with Jackson following behind.

—Dad

Easter

Dear Sarah,

TOMORROW IS EASTER. THIS IS THE HIGH HOLY DAY FOR CHRISTIANS throughout the world. Yesterday we commemorated the crucifixion of Jesus on what we call Good Friday. The early church originally designated the Friday of Jesus' crucifixion as Great, Holy, or Good Friday. The origin of the term is not certain, but some scholars posit that it came from the idea of Jesus' crucifixion occurring on "God's Friday."

Whatever the derivation, the day is well named because it became good only because God brought good out of the worst possible crime. I didn't begin to understand how anything good could come from the state's execution of a sinless man, until I experienced personally the depth of the apostle Paul's truth in these words: "We know that in everything God works for good with those who love him" (Romans 8:28 RSV).

Without the miracle of Easter, Good Friday would simply be another black mark on the sad and sordid history of the human race, which, since creation, has been driven by fear and been too often blind to the saving power of love. But Easter is not only about the resurrection of one perfect man, it is even more about God's annual proclamation of the liberation of every human being from fear's grip.

Easter arrives each spring to remind us with natural symbols and through a penetrating and always mystical knowing that restoration is every human being's destiny, no matter our motivations, our level of faith, or our awareness of the need for being saved from something. Easter is love's ultimate victory because love always has the final word over death and everything else that scares us.

By the time Luke wrote the Acts of the Apostles, the early church expected a day to come when everyone would be restored. In a speech recorded in the third chapter (verse 21) of Acts, Peter refers to what he terms a time of "universal restoration." This idea, more than any other I've ever encountered, points emphatically to the real meaning underlying our celebration of Easter.

The cross of Jesus of Nazareth became our most sacred symbol because love willed that the day of his crucifixion be forever redeemed. Love transformed that tragic afternoon from humanity's biggest fear-induced mistake into what we today know as Good Friday.

Easter comes tomorrow not so a special few who claim to believe the so-called right doctrines and precepts can celebrate. This new day will break upon the whole of humanity to proclaim in the majesty of silence and light the incontrovertible truth that love is the victor over every human being's long, personal, and always painful bondage to fear. Universal restoration, then, is the true message of Easter.

I am amused when I hear others tell me that they don't "get" Easter. When they ask me if I believe in resurrection, I smile before I say, "I not only believe in it, I've seen it."

"Seen it?" they asked incredulously. And that's when I report that I am a witness to Easter every time I see a life delivered from fear and fully restored so that it can become the fullest possible expression of what it means to love. Three hundred and sixty-five days a year all over this planet, men and women experience their own personal resurrections every time they walk out of a twelve-step meeting committed to giving their addiction to the God of their own understanding. And every time a human being makes the courageous decision to put love before one more fear-driven expression of the self, Easter happens. For each time love is invited into a wounded life to exorcise the darkness of fear, resurrection follows.

Easter happens every day because love is both our source and our destiny. What the Christian world will formally celebrate tomorrow in church sanctuaries and on hillsides at sunrise is the glorious symbol of God's amazing gift to every human being regardless of anything and in spite of everything. And to that I offer a humble "Hallelujah!"

—Dad

Pious Idolatry

Dear Sarah,

MOST OF US HUMAN BEINGS SEEM TO POSSESS WHAT OUR BUDDHIST brothers and sisters term a "clinging mind." This means that when something becomes very important to us, we are immediately tempted to elevate it to the status of deity. Sadly, many Christians have done this with Scripture to the point that they much prefer to believe that every word of the Bible is what some call the "breathed" Word of God. And in believing this, they come to so revere Scripture that they unconsciously make it the fourth person of the Godhead.

I respect and love Scripture, but, thank God, I learned in seminary thirty years ago to read it as a body of "inspired" literature, much of which evolved out of several ancient oral traditions. Every word of Scripture was written by a human being who was struggling at some level to give order to humanity's interface with Mystery. This was a daunting task, especially for a prescientific people with, as was the case of the Hebrews, an unsophisticated worldview.

Recently, I was requested to write a series of devotionals that were "published" on the Internet. In one of those pieces, I made reference to the story of Abraham taking Isaac up the mountain, and I referred to this story as a folktale, which is precisely what it is. Technically, the story is a myth, as is much of the prehistory in the Old Testament.

The E-mail I received were filled with vitriol in reaction to my characterization of this story as nonhistorical. It was as though I had attacked the divinity of Christ or had written something so scandalous that I deserved to be severely reprimanded.

I had forgotten how frightened many people are and how they cling to black-and-white belief systems that they believe will somehow protect them from a threatening universe. These are so-called good Christian folk, but in my view, they are tragically frightened people who stand in sore need of letting go of the false god of their subjective view of Scripture so that they might come to discover the great truths of faith.

All real truth must be discovered; therefore, it is not my place to instruct those who don't ask for it. But it is definitely my place to love, forgive, and, on occasion, even turn the other cheek to those who would do me harm because of my insistence upon discovering truth.

—Dad

Benediction

Dear Sarah,

AN UNSEASONABLY COLD BREEZE SHOOK THE FEW BLUEBONNETS that elected to show themselves in that broad expanse of meadow separating the Pedernales River from a rocky hill. Last year this patch of earth was transformed by April into a carpet of blue waves, but this new season is a far different matter. Perhaps it was a late freeze or then again possibly insufficient autumn rains, but whatever the cause, the flowers are in no way profuse. Their fragrance is faint and their glory diminished.

But still they have returned to instruct me in lessons too deep for words. Love remains their proclamation, hope, their purpose. As I step amidst their sparse beauty, the wind pronounces a benediction over this vigil and gives birth to a light that burns warmly within my soul. And I thank God for these little azure visitors, but even more for a promise that never fades or falters. This work is finished, but apparently I am not.

—Dad

Amen.

Epilogue

SIX MONTHS AFTER MY INITIAL DIAGNOSIS OF CONGESTIVE HEART failure, I agreed to speak at St. Matthew's Episcopal Church, here in Austin, at their 2002 Wednesday evening Lenten services. I showed up that night fatigued and more than a little preoccupied with my health because in five days I would undergo an echocardiogram that would, I was told, determine if the prescribed medicine had proved effective. I told myself that I felt better, although I was still very tired; and preaching and teaching in evening services had for the last six months been ruled out altogether by my physician. *Rest* and *exercise* was his simple two-word mandate following my release from the hospital. Consequently, I said no to every invitation, but I could not bring myself to turn down the good people of St. Matthew's. My literary agent, Kathleen Davis Niendorff, who is one of God's true lights, had invited me with the caveat that if I didn't feel up to it, I could back out even at the last minute. Further, J. Keith Miller, my good friend and one of this country's best-loved spiritual writers, was scheduled to introduce me. How could I pass up this opportunity? I could not.

I spoke for about forty-five minutes and, to my surprise, received a standing ovation. As much as anything, those present were applauding my willingness to show up and speak under difficult circumstances. Following the closing prayer, I greeted the people and received a flood of good wishes and sincere promises for prayer.

That's when it happened: A shy young woman I scarcely knew approached me and reintroduced herself. Immediately I remembered her. She requested permission to pray for me. "Sure!" was my response. To my astonishment, not to mention embarrassment, she placed her hand upon my forehead and began to pray out loud. I couldn't get out of this situation fast enough. In seminary, thirty years before, I had seen a professor dismissed from the faculty because of his preoccupation with faith healing and other supposed gifts of the Spirit. Consequently, I had made the decision in that first year of theological education never to dabble in the mystical, at least not in public. As I was taught to understand Holiness, God was, for the most part, an interesting intellectual proposition whose Being might best be expressed in the one-hundred-dollar words we were taught to use in the seminary. Thirty years ago, we talked a lot *about* God but seldom directly *to* God; but on this unforgettable night, this saint, whose name is Sandy Lanier, talked directly to God as I trembled.

When her prayer was done, I thanked her and walked outside into the cool early spring evening, grateful to have the obligation of speaking behind me. Five days later, I entered the heart clinic with no small amount of trepidation, and I did my best to read the eyes of the young woman who administered the test. "You can't tell me anything, can you?" I asked.

"No sir," she replied, "but Dr. Lowe will read the results and write you a letter."

Write me a letter! I thought. *A man is going to read the results off a machine and write me a letter regarding whether or not I get to stay in this life.* I shrugged, said, "Okay," and returned to work.

When I arrived home, Dr. George Lowe, who is an extraordinary physician, whose commitment to medicine is exceeded only by his love of God and his fellow human beings, called me at home and left this voice mail message: "Dr. Lively, I have read your results. You have been covered by grace. Your heart has returned to normal functioning." Dr. Lowe knew nothing of the prayer Sandy had offered. Six months later, after yet another echocardiogram, Dr. Lowe placed the video of my heart into the monitor, turned the VCR on, pointed to the image of my pulsating heart, and said, "That is a beautiful heart. This is what people pray for." Again, I had yet to tell him of Sandy's prayer.

What I have described above is what happened as best I know to tell of it. I can't explain it, and I am sufficiently wise not to try. But to write that I appreciate this "miracle" is to understate woefully the depth of my gratitude. What the astonishing result of Sandy Lanier's prayer means is that I get to live for a while longer—and, therefore, I now have the opportunity to express love in so many new and wonderful ways and even in ways that before my illness I never realized might be possible for me.

Not long ago, Dr. Lowe asked me what I learned from all of this. He framed his question this way: "In the American Civil War, soldiers would say, 'I've seen the elephant.' This meant they'd seen combat and death, firsthand and up close." He continued, "You have now seen the elephant. So what did you learn from the experience?" I didn't have to think long to supply an answer. I responded, "I've learned that this life is a truly incredible gift that has never actually been about me." He smiled knowingly with that certain twinkle in his eye that signaled understanding.

This epilogue would not be complete without a personal word from the saint who prayed for me. When I heard that this collection of letters, *Waiting for Bluebonnets*, was going to be published, I requested that Sandy Lanier record her memory of that evening she willingly and so faithfully prayed for me. What follows is her insightful response to that request:

I well remember that night. I was not in a good place emotionally. I had felt shame when I had shared with Bob what I had written during his classes. I felt like that was the wrong thing to do. I felt awed by him and, with my background, less than him. So I just quit going to his class and decided I would never see or talk to him again.

Then I found out Bob was coming to St. Matthew's to speak. I knew it would be good. But I felt that going would cause me to feel all the inferiority, even shame, again—all of those "less than" feelings. But I knew it would be a wonderful talk. So I decided to go but sit in the back. I would not speak to him afterward.

Bob is a wonderful storyteller, and he used a humorous story to illustrate the grace of God in a way that touched me deeply. I was shocked, however, by the difference in Bob's appearance. He looked gray and so much older than his years. His change in appearance had seemed to happen so quickly. I had seen him less than a year ago, and the difference was shocking. I thought he looked like "walking death." I felt so much compassion. But I had got myself there by vowing not to speak to him. Then I decided I would just say hello. The church was clearing out. I met Bob as he was coming down the aisle; I did not expect him to remember me, but he did. I am not even sure I commented on his talk, which normally would have been the first thing I said. Out of my mouth, like it was not even me, came words such as You've been really sick *or something like that. And part of me was thinking,* Boy that was tactful.

Then I said to him, "I will pray for you." And I think he said something about thank you and he needed prayers. And then to my astonishment, out of my mouth came these words. "Could I pray for you right now?" He said, "Yes." I think I put my hand on top of his head. And I prayed. I do not remember one word that I prayed; however, I never do remember what I say when I pray. For as always, when I pray, it is not about me; it is about God and the one I pray for. The words are not mine. I cease to exist while I am praying for someone else. It is the easiest and the hardest thing I do.

After the prayer, I told Bob I would continue to pray for him; and I left. I could not believe what I had just done. I was not even sure what had come over me. It was as if something propelled me forward when I was wanting to leave. However, I continued to pray for Bob every day.

As time went on, I began to reflect on what it means to be obedient, and how what so many people would say is faith may actually have more to do with obedience. After I spoke to Bob this week, I again reflected on obedience. And it has occurred to me that while Bob had given a beautiful talk on grace, he actually was visited by healing grace that evening.

In conclusion, I give thanks to the emergency room physician who first diagnosed my disease; to Dr. George Lowe, who treated me following the emergency-room diagnosis; to Sandy Lanier, who dared to pray for me when neither of us was comfortable with the idea; and most of all to God, who has given me more days to live so that I might experience even more the truth that love never ends.

Bob Lively